The ACT Guide to Managing Liquidity

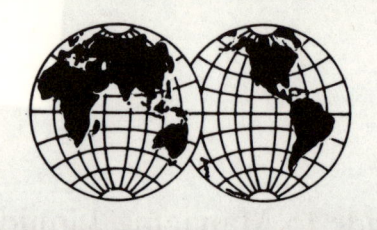

Euro Brokers

Euro Brokers is delighted to be associated with the publication of *The ACT Guide to Managing Liquidity*. The Association has the highest reputation for promoting professionalism in the field of treasury management which includes its educational programmes. This book represents a major contribution to the pool of knowledge of treasury procedures for both experienced practitioners and students.

Liquidity management is one of the fundamentals in ensuring the financial well-being of an organization. Euro Brokers' expertise and experience in this area puts us in a privileged position to appreciate the importance of and need for a textbook of the highest standard. This criterion has been achieved admirably.

Our strategy at Euro Brokers is to provide organizations with a comprehensive treasury service supported by technical expertise, innovation and professionalism. Working together with the Association on the publication of this book gives us the greatest pleasure, particularly in view of our common objectives.

Euro Brokers Financial Services Limited

ACT

The ACT Guide to Managing Liquidity

Lance Moir

BLACKWELL
Finance

Copyright © Lance Moir 1992

First published 1992

Blackwell Publishers
108 Cowley Road
Oxford OX4 1JF
UK

238 Main street
Suite 501
Cambridge, Massachusetts 02142
USA

All rights reserved. Except for the quotation of short passages for the purposes of criticism and review, no part of this publication may be reproduced, stored in a retrieval system, or transmitted, in any form or by any means, electronic, mechanical, photocopying, recording or otherwise, without the prior permission of the publisher.

Except in the United States of America, this book is sold subject to the condition that it shall not, by way of trade or otherwise, be lent, resold, hired out, or otherwise circulated without the publisher's prior consent in any form of binding or cover other than that in which it is published and without a similar condition including this condition being imposed on the subsequent purchaser.

British Library Cataloguing in Publication Data

A CIP catalogue record for this book is available from the British Library.

Library of Congress Cataloging-in-Publication Data
Moir, Lance.
    The ACT guide to managing liquidity / Lance Moir.
      p. cm.
    Includes bibliographical references and index.
    1. Cash management. 2. Liquidity (Economics) 3. Corporations– –Finance. 4. International business enterprises—Finance.
I. Title.
HG4028.C45M65   1992
658.15'244—dc20
                                          92–20996
                                             CIP

ISBN 0-631-187367

Typeset in 12 on 14pt Baskerville by TecSet Ltd

Printed in Great Britain by T.J. Press (Padstow) Ltd, Padstow, Cornwall.

This book is printed on acid-free paper

Contents

List of Figures	vi
List of Tables	vii
Foreword by Daniel Hodson	viii
Preface	ix
1 What is Liquidity and How does it arise?	1
2 Forecasting Liquidity	9
3 The Management of Uncertainty	29
4 The Structure of Interest Rates and the Yield Curve	39
5 Managing your Bank and Bank Services	53
6 Liquidity and the Use of Deposit and Borrowing Instruments	69
7 Managing Interest Rate Risk	83
8 Liquidity Management in Practice	97
9 Organizing Liquidity Management	115
Glossary	121
Appendix 1 Useful Calculations	131
Appendix 2 Sample ACT Examination Questions	133
List of Further Reading	169
Index	155

List of Figures

1.1	A normal working cash cycle	6
3.1	A typical variance analysis	32
4.1	Normal yield curve	43
4.2	Flat yield curve	44
4.3	Inverse yield curve	45
7.1	Caps, floors and collars	90
7.2	Interest rate collar	91
8.1	The process of liquidity management	99
8.2	Seasonal PLC: total cash forecasts	101

List of Tables

2.1	Jackets Limited: financial information	11
2.2	Jackets Limited: cash flow	12
2.3	Basic format of receipts and payments method	16
2.4	Format of receipts and payments method for a group	18
2.5	Format for source and application method	21
3.1	Seasonal PLC: cash forecasts	31
4.1	Various APRs compared with quoted rates	50
5.1	National Westminster Bank PLC interest apportionment service	63
5.2	A netting system	64
5.3	Zero-balancing	65
5.4	NatWest BankLine Plus balance report	67
5.5	NatWest BankLine Plus previous day transaction report	68
6.1	Use of overdrafts	77
8.1	Seasonal PLC: cash forecasts	100
8.2	Seasonal PLC: current interest rates	103
8.3	International Cruises Inc.: cash forecasts	106
8.4	D and L Engineering: past 3 months' figures	110
A2.1	Cash flow forecast for MMS contract	134

A2.2	Selected balance sheet data for Group companies, year ended 31.8.91 and budgeted for the year to 31.8.92	139
A2.3	Budgeted profit and loss account data for the year to 31.8.92	140
A2.4	Summary capital budgets of UK operating companies	140
A2.5	Cash flow forecasts for the three companies for the year ending 31.8.92	142
A2.6	Basic ratios	143
A2.7	Financial information	146
A2.8	Speculative PLC: profit and loss account for the year ended 30.6.89	149

Foreword

Education and the pursuit of excellence in treasury management are the principal objectives of the Association of Corporate Treasurers. This, the first book specifically commissioned by the Association as part of a series of guides to the Treasury subjects, is intended to fulfil these objectives at every professional level; for the finance director as a reference book in which to dip, for the aspiring treasurer as a means to enhance his general knowledge, and for the student as a solid foundation on which to build. We also hope that it will be of practical use to more non-financial managers who wish to improve their financial literacy.

Cash is at the head of every business, and is the daily stock in trade of the treasurer. Liquidity Management is therefore a highly appropriate title for the first ACT guide and we are very fortunate in Lance Moir to have an author who is well placed to write in-depth on the subject. Lance has been involved in the Association's education programme virtually since its inception, and gained his ACT Diploma of Corporate Treasury Management in 1986, with the first group of successful candidates. Since then he has had a distinguished career as a corporate treasurer, and is uniquely qualified to blend practical experience with academic principles.

I'm also delighted that we've been able to work with Euro Brokers in producing this book. The Association recognizes with gratitude their contribution to the development of treasury expertise.

This important guide covers a vital topic in a concise, readable format, but without losing depth or sophistication. I am sure that it will become essential reading and will be of great practical use to all those whose career takes on treasury management. I commend it warmly to readers.

Daniel Hodson
(Deputy Chief Executive and Group Finance Director of Nationwide Building Society, the current President of the Association of Corporate Treasurers and immediate past Chairman of the ACT Publications Committee.)

Preface

This book has been written in order to describe how the basic management of liquidity operates in companies – both domestic and multinational. In particular, it attempts to set some of the basic decisions in liquidity management (how much do I deposit, for how long and at what rate) in the overall business context.

However, it does not claim to be a complete study of liquidity. In particular, the details of money transmission, debtor and creditor control and international trade finance are excluded, while there is only a rudimentary examination of short-term deposit and borrowing instruments.

It is written not only for the student of treasury management, but also for non-financial executives who need to know what liquidity management is all about. It should also be useful for the small business person who will meet the concepts of liquidity management every day.

Liquidity is only part of treasury management, and so certain problems which arise from a lack of liquidity naturally lead directly on to the ability to raise debt and other issues. Funding management and corporate finance and these developments are deliberately beyond the scope of this book. Nevertheless, surrounding events have to be considered when

Preface

applying any liquidity management technique, but I hope that this book places liquidity management in the general business context and will be suitable both for the treasury specialist and general business person alike.

Appendix 2 includes some past ACT examination questions in liquidity management together with possible answers. (Note that there can be no single correct answer as there is usually always a range of possible approaches to any given situation.)

I am grateful to the Association of Corporate Treasurers for pushing me to write this book and to the administrative staff of the ACT, especially Gay Pierpoint, who are always a constant source of help. My particular thanks to Andrew McMillan who kept me on the straight and narrow and provided many helpful comments and suggestions. Also to Michael Bryant and Gerry Leahy for their comments on early drafts.

However, my greatest thanks go to David Ireland who trudged through the first drafts, improving my English and assuring me that certain paragraphs, if not changed, would be incomprehensible to all but mind-readers.

Lance Moir

1
What is Liquidity and How does it Arise?

- The definition of liquidity
- The broad objectives of liquidity management
- How liquidity impacts on a business

What is Liquidity?

The liquidity of an organization is the ability to make payments as they fall due. Perhaps, more importantly, are the consequences of *illiquidity* which are likely to lead to a business ceasing to trade.

A company may be highly profitable in an accounting sense, but this is of no use if there is no cash to pay employees and suppliers and no cash to make further investments. Conversely, a company which is making large accounting losses may be generating substantial cash (e.g. early in the 1980s Courtaulds made substantial accounting losses, yet generated millions of pounds before repaying loans and paying dividends).

Although the availability of liquidity to a company is the prime objective, that liquidity also requires active management in order to benefit the company in a financial sense, but also to avoid and minimize risk.

What is Liquidity and How does it Arise?

The scope of liquidity management usually extends to the control of:

- cash flow and cash flow forecasting;
- investments and borrowings of up to 1 year;
- availability of borrowing facilities;
- interest rate management.

It will also cover detailed applications including money transmission, and debtor and creditor management.

How does Liquidity Arise?

In order to manage effectively a company's liquidity, it is important to understand how it arises and the uses that it is put to. In particular, there is a need to understand the dynamics of the business, particularly in so far as these affect the cash flow. For example, as sales grow, how much extra cash is consumed by working capital (or, for large food retailers, how much cash is generated).

As part of the normal business cycle, liquidity arises:

1 By generating profits in cash terms; that is, through selling goods for cash in excess of that required to produce them. This will be made up of a number of cash flows, both in and out:
(a) cash sales;
(b) receipts from debtors;
(c) payments to creditors;
(d) operating costs;
(e) capital invested;
(f) dividend and interest payments.
Naturally it follows that if the business is either growing or inefficient, then liquidity is consumed rather than generated.

What is Liquidity and How does it Arise?

2 By selling for cash assets that are no longer necessary.
3 By raising funds (either debt or equity) in excess of the amount needed for investment by the company at that time. This might typically happen where a company has a planned expansion programme and decides that it would be prudent to raise the necessary finance in advance (e.g. pharmaceutical development or oil exploration).

Liquidity is consumed:

1 By making new investments in fixed assets, or acquiring businesses.
2 By increasing working capital in order to expand sales or improve margins.
3 By making losses in excess of the depreciation charge.

These are the factors which affect liquidity over a long-term business cycle, but on a day-to-day basis, more significant factors are likely to be receipts and major payments to suppliers or for payroll. For many small businesses, it is items such as these which really represent liquidity.

It is important to note the emphasis on cash in the above lists. The amount of cash available can be measured unambiguously, whereas other accounting treatments can be more subjective. The amount of cash used in working capital is particularly important and in situations of illiquidity it is often working capital which can be squeezed first to generate liquidity, where other assets will take longer to realize.

What are the Objectives of Liquidity Management?

The sheer importance of continuing liquidity to a business has led to a very strong trend towards centralization of cash

What is Liquidity and How does it Arise?

and general treasury management within groups. The small business always has to concentrate on cash flow, and this is also true in the largest multinational group.

The prime objectives of liquidity management are:

1 *Liquidity*. The business must be able to meet its liabilities as they fall due.
2 *Safety*. Investments should not be exposed to the risk of an unacceptable loss in capital value, and borrowing facilities should continue to be available when needed (i.e. there is no point in having borrowing facilities available if the prospective lender is about to fail).
3 *Profitability*. Only once it is certain that the first two objectives can be met, can the question of return be considered. There will always be a trade-off between risk and reward, but there must also be a clear view of how much risk the business is prepared to accept and whether the reward is enough to compensate.

Once these objectives have been satisfied, flexibility may also enter the picture. Whereas the availability of liquidity should always be considered for the range of likely business events, there may also be alternatives available in the selection of deposit instruments or interest periods. All other things being equal, the more flexible alternative will always be more desirable.

Liquidity in Different Industries

While the ultimate objective of ensuring that there is enough cash to pay the bills is the same across all businesses, the nature of the industry will change the way in which it is operated. Clearly, the amount of equity and debt in any given

What is Liquidity and How does it Arise?

company should reflect the needs of the business and no amount of good liquidity management will be able to compensate for a basic deficiency in the capital structure.

First, suppose that we are running a market stall selling fruit and vegetables. Each day, we will sell for cash and because the product will rot if not sold, we are unlikely to have any significant stock. Equally, we will buy our goods for sale each day, probably from a wholesaler. The ideal position here would be to try to obtain some credit from the wholesaler, but this may only be possible if we are able to offer perhaps a guarantee or when reliable trading has been established. Here, liquidity is very much a day-to-day matter, particularly if any additional staff are employed who need paying on a regular basis.

Alternatively, if the business in which we are involved is a company purely researching into pharmaceuticals, with no products foreseeable for some years, then the business will not get very far unless it has enough capital in the form of cash to last for some years. In this case, liquidity becomes a matter of conserving cash and using the strength of high levels of cash to negotiate longer periods for credit taken. Then, there is an opportunity to manage interest income by selecting different periods in which to deposit.

But if we look at more complex groups of businesses, there is a distinct need to understand the cash generation cycle in detail. The larger capital elements such as capital expenditure, new equity or the payment of tax and dividends are readily identifiable, but the cash flows in the working capital cycle need closer examination. The working capital cash cycle is the timing difference between the purchase of raw materials and receipt of cash from their sale after processing. In addition, further costs involved need to be examined. Different businesses will be affected in different ways. Supermarket chains, for example, may have a negative cash cycle as they

What is Liquidity and How does it Arise?

often pay for goods well after they have sold to the public. If, however, the business is a food company supplying a major supermarket, then a decision by the supermarket to take (say) 3 days' more credit could have an impact of millions of pounds in the suppliers.

A normal working cash cycle (i.e. where the cash involved is positive) might be depicted as in Figure 1.1.

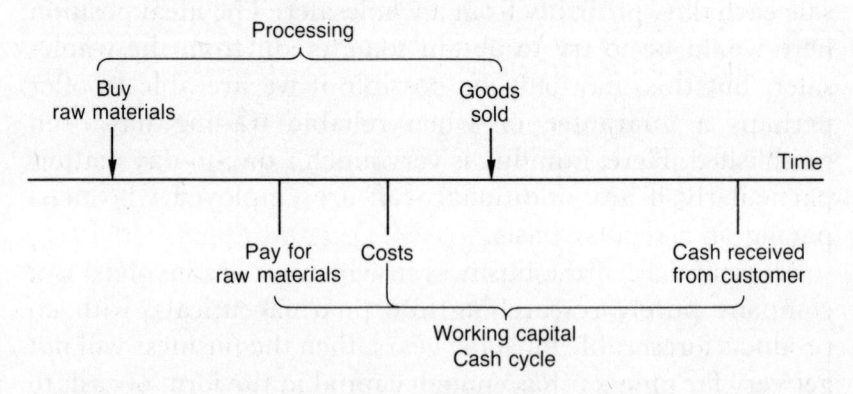

Figure 1.1 A normal working cash cycle

Let us consider the broad liquidity issues of three different businesses: food manufacturing, fashion retailing and heavy engineering.

A food manufacturer

Once the purchase of capital equipment has been established, the working capital cycle will be critical. The timing of the purchase of raw materials may be dictated by availability of supply, whereas the sale of finished products may be dictated by an entirely different market, possibly in different countries. The importance of credit periods taken by customers has already been noted and systems will need to be in place to identify changes.

A fashion retailer

As opposed to a food retailer, a fashion retailer will again be dependent on the working capital cycle. Goods will be ordered and paid for in advance of sale (possibly before they are even in the shops if they are imported). Therefore, there will be the cash consumed both by advance payment and by stockholding. Cash will then be received when the goods are sold. Unlike a food manufacturer, therefore, the individual elements of payments to suppliers and receipts from sales will need to be monitored separately (in a business where sales and purchases are more closely connected, it might be possible to monitor the net position). Additionally, the seasonality of this type of business means that each month will need to be considered individually.

A heavy engineering company

Clearly the initial capital investment in plant and machinery is going to be the most significant item in this type of company. After that, the liquidity management once more centres on control of working capital and operating costs. Accounting systems will be based upon depreciating capital equipment and may show large losses which disguise the cash movements. Raw materials will be bought on credit, but the manufacturing process may mean that large amounts of cash are tied up in work-in-progress (and this figure will increase with very large items such as aircraft engines). Finished stock may then also be held for long periods and, although no cash may actually be moving at this point, liquidity may continue to be consumed if further products continue to be manufactured. Finally sales will probably be made on credit and

What is Liquidity and How does it Arise?

control of the period extended will be needed. In this instance, the amount tied up in working capital may not only be significant, but unlike the retailer, it is also illiquid. This means that working capital in this type of business needs to be financed from longer-term sources of finance.

So in this way (and in many others) different industries lead to different ways of managing liquidity.

2
Forecasting Liquidity

- The importance of the cash forecast
- Different methods of preparing the cash forecast
- Problems that arise in practice

The Importance of the Cash Forecast

As has been explained in chapter 1, the availability of cash to meet liabilities as they fall due is central to the continued existence of businesses. In order to be certain about the availability of cash and how to manage it, there is a need to prepare cash forecasts on a regular basis. One way to ensure liquidity is to maintain large cash balances or arrange necessary borrowing facilities, which may be expensive, but neither of these approaches will result in optimal profitability. Therefore, reliable cash forecasts are essential in order to minimize idle cash balances and reduce loan costs and hence improve results.

Cash forecasts are normally prepared on three time scales:

1. The very short-term forecast, which looks at likely cash flow over the next few days; this includes cheques drawn and about to be received through the banking system, as well as cash receipts and other known payments. This ought to be fairly accurate.

Forecasting Liquidity

2 The short- to medium-term forecast, looking about 6 months forward. This gives the general shape of the cash flow and allows various alternative funding and investment decisions to be made.
3 The long-term forecast, looking at perhaps 4 or 5 years (or even longer in major capital-intensive industries). This is, in effect, the cash element of the corporate plan and will form the basis of the funding strategy.

The way that cash forecasts are designed will depend on the structure of the company and the nature of its business. However, any cash forecast will be prepared in order to show the following:

- the amount of cash surplus or requirement;
- when the cash surplus or requirement will arise;
- how long the cash surplus or requirement will last;
- how the cash will eventually be used or generated;
- in what currency the cash will be available or needed.

Consider the company Jackets Limited (table 2.1). This is a company which has been expanding fast, but has high and growing profit margins. To the outside world, it seems as if it is a good credit risk to its suppliers. Yet, the amount of trade credit has expanded.

Ostensibly, the ratio of debt to equity is within reasonable limits, yet the company has available borrowing facilities of only £500,000 which are on a demand basis and fall due for review 3 months after the year-end.

When we add the information that the accounts are prepared at the year-end, which represents a low point in cash terms ahead of seasonal stock requirements, we can see how little use formal accounts are in the liquidity management of a business (table 2.2). (Note: these cashflows have been summarized to show the total picture.)

Forecasting Liquidity

Table 2.1 Jackets Limited: financial information

	Year			
	X1	X2	X3	X4
Sales (£000)	586	921	2204	3937
Profit before tax (£000)	21	107	406	616
Gross margin (%)	39.9	43.3	47.3	49.7
Net margin (%)	3.6	11.6	18.4	15.6
Earnings per share (p)	0.28	1.02	4.15	6.22
Balance sheet (£000)				
Fixed assets	89	178	453	1027
Stock	77	196	484	971
Debtors	10	31	49	129
Cash	1	1	1	1
Bank overdraft	(31)	(41)	(49)	(225)
Trade creditors	(43)	(103)	(211)	(519)
Other creditors	(36)	(100)	(158)	(210)
Taxation	(8)	(39)	(192)	(352)
Long-term creditors	(6)	(4)	(6)	(95)
Provisions	(8)	(15)	(18)	(16)
Net assets	45	104	353	711
Creditors/sales × 360	26	40	34	47
Stock/sales × 360	47	77	79	89
Debt/net assets × 100	69	39	14	32

But if we extend the forecast by a further year and assume some physical expansion, we can see that the company cannot continue to grow without a significant injection of capital. This demonstrates the importance of attention to cash flow forecasts in the management of business.

This forecast has been prepared on an annual basis. If we were to look more closely at the next 3 months, we would see

Forecasting Liquidity

Table 2.2 Jackets Limited: cash flow

	X4	X5 (forecast)[a]
Profit	616	700
Add: Non-cash	129	175
	745	875
Increase in stock	(487)	(600)
Increase in debtors	(80)	(100)
Increase in creditors	360	450
Tax paid	(85)	(175)
Operating cash flow	453	450
Capital expenditure	(717)	(750)
Dividends	(15)	(15)
Disposal of assets	14	0
Other	(4)	0
Net cash flow	(269)	(335)

[a] The forecast for year X5 assumes further expansion at the current rate and also assumes the continued willingness of suppliers to advance credit.

that the seasonality of the business leads to growing stock during that period. Unless trade credit can be extended to an extreme level, the company will not be able to continue to trade because of lack of raw materials. So what looked like a long-term problem may become a short-term crisis which may give the owners of the business few options. In fact what seemed like a need to raise either equity or long-term debt to finance expansion becomes a crisis of how to continue to trade over the coming months. The eventual reality of this situation was a need to find nearly £1 million to satisfy pressing creditors and was only resolved by a quick sale of the business. Thus the lack of clear planning arising from timely cash forecasts reduced the options available to the business.

It is clear that the absence of timely cash flow forecasts obstructed any planning and reduced the options available, whereas the preparation of such forecasts would have allowed the management to take well-planned decisions. It would also have given them the confidence to persuade bankers and investors to support the company. Most importantly, it would have allowed them options which might not have been available in a crisis.

Uses of Cash Forecasts

Before considering the techniques of preparing cash forecasts, it is useful to review their end uses. If these are considered at an early stage, then the particular form of any report prepared can be designed in advance. It will also allow the necessary degree of accuracy and frequency of the forecast to be taken into account:

1 Short term:
   (a) advance warning of liquidity problems;
   (b) availability of funds to make payments;
   (c) level of funds available to deposit;
   (d) shortfall in funds to be borrowed;
   (e) confirmation of short-term trading forecasts.
2 Medium term:
   (a) funding and depositing profile;
   (b) exposure to interest rate and currency risk.
3 Long term:
   (a) funding strategy;
   (b) major investment decisions;

(c) ability to meet corporate objectives and dividend policy;
(d) exposure to interest rate and currency risk.

The basic format can be prepared at business unit/individual company level and then consolidated for group purposes at the required level of detail. For example, in decentralized groups it may be enough to consolidate the flows of individual companies and then add group movements. In other situations it may be more appropriate to separate out capital expenditure and other cash flows which do not arise from day-to-day trading. These alternatives are discussed in greater detail later in this chapter.

Preparation of the Cash Forecast

There are two main methods of preparing cash forecasts – the receipts and payments method and the source and application method. They tend to be applicable to different situations and are complementary rather than direct alternatives.

In both cases, prior to consolidation on a group basis, each forecast should be prepared by major currency and major legal entity. Note the emphasis on major – there is no need to spend so much time preparing forecasts that there is no time to act upon them. As much effort as is required to provide all meaningful information should be spent, bearing in mind the cost of preparation, but no more.

The receipts and payments method

At its most basic, this involves listing all the receipts which are expected to be received during the forecast period and

Forecasting Liquidity

deducting the payments expected to be made. This net flow is then added to the opening position to give a forecast closing position.

If you were to attempt to prepare a personal cash forecast for the coming month, this might be done by starting with your opening bank balance, adding salary and other receipts and then deducting mortgage payments or rent, cost of food and travel etc. to give a closing bank balance for the end of the month. Preparation of a company's cash forecast takes this same basic principle into a business context.

A basic format might look like that given in table 2.3. This basic forecast would be prepared at business-unit level. Therefore, not all the categories would be appropriate (such as dividends) and it may be desirable to introduce others. It would be necessary to define first the period(s) to be forecast and the level of detail required (e.g. hundreds, thousands of relevant currency).

Points to note:

- All figures are *cash*, so sales does not mean all sales, just those made in cash. But receipts in cash from sales made in a previous period are included.
- Similarly, all costs and payments to suppliers are not included, only those made *in cash*, but payments to creditors in the current period are included.
- It is often useful to try to list inter-company payments separately, as group analysis will be particularly interested in external cash flow.

This forecast is likely to be prepared by a cashier's department and so may not include payments under the control of more senior management. Therefore, controls will be needed to ensure that all known major payments are covered by the forecast at some level.

Forecasting Liquidity

Table 2.3 Basic format of receipts and payments method

	Period 1	Period 2
Opening balance		
Receipts		
Sales in cash		
Receipts from debtors		
Sale of assets in cash		
Tax receipts		
Other receipts		
Inter-company receipts		
Total receipts		
Payments		
Suppliers in cash		
Wages		
Rent		
Utilities		
Other costs		
Capital expenditure		
Dividends		
Tax		
Other		
Inter-company payments		
Total payments		
Net movement		
Closing balance		

Forecasting Liquidity

While normal trading payments are generally well controlled and therefore forecast, one-off payments such as major asset sales and items of capital expenditure are often forgotten – usually because 'everyone knew about it'. Therefore, for critical forecasts such as a daily one for the next few days, the end-user of the forecast will have to consider carefully whether all major payments are included.

In a group, the individual forecasts will be consolidated to produce a combined trading position. The group treasury department will then need to add the treasury transactions to produce the net figure available for investment or to be borrowed over the period. Such a format might be as that given in table 2.4. This format does not differ in concept from that used by the trading business, but concentrates on the payments made by or to a central treasury department. These payments should tie in to the diary system which should be maintained by any treasury department. Care will be needed to ensure that any receipts or payments included in the trading flows are not duplicated in the treasury forecasts.

Particular notes are:

- As with the trading forecasts, care needs to be exercised that all payments are cash payments, e.g. interest.
- Individual forecasts should be prepared by currency, therefore foreign exchange means cash flows in *that* currency. This may mean that there is a corresponding flow in a different currency cash forecast.
- 'Other' may include items like option premia, FRA settlements (see chapter 7).
- Tax and dividends may be necessary given the increasing use of separate companies for treasury functions, but again care should be exercised to ensure the matching flow is reflected if payments are intra-group.
- Care should be exercised to ensure that there is clear treatment of loan roll-overs. In particular, it is often better to show

Forecasting Liquidity

Table 2.4 Format of receipts and payments method for a group

	Period 1	Period 2
Opening position		
Receipts		
Trading flow		
Maturing investments		
Interest income		
Foreign exchange		
New borrowings		
Other		
Total receipts		
Payments		
New investments		
Interest payments		
Foreign exchange		
Dividends		
Tax		
Maturing borrowings		
Other		
Total payments		
Net movement		
Closing position		

these as a repayment and fresh borrowing. This will allow a clearer decision to be made on the period of the new borrowing.

Limitations of the receipts and payments method

The receipts and payments method of forecasting is very good for short periods. It can often be tied in to known cheque runs or receipts from sales already made. However, the technique of forecasting the cash position from individual items means that these items are considered in isolation from each other, therefore a particular bias in one figure can lead to a nonsense over a longer forecast. For example, if a conservative approach is taken to future sales (and this is often very sensible), then a forecast read on this basis over a year may lead to a ridiculously high stock position. Equally, the consideration of cost items individually may result in a ridiculously high or low profit result. This is because this method looks at cash in a different way from the main accounting systems, precisely by not considering accounting-driven terms such as profit or stock levels.

Therefore, over longer periods it is often more useful to use the source and application method of forecasting cash. The principal use of this method is that it ties in to normal financial control systems and can be used to set clearer objectives for operational management.

The source and application method

Whereas the starting-point of the receipts and payments method is sales, the source and application method starts with profit. Therefore, a considerable number of assumptions have already been made and should already have been

Forecasting Liquidity

scrutinized by the responsible operational management and the appropriate level of financial controller. This issue is considered in greater detail in Chapter 3.

Before describing the format and technique of preparing this forecast, it is important to stress that this is *not* the same as the source and application of funds statements under UK accounting standards. The accounting standard is an expression of accounting movements in a format which some managements use to hide the underlying cash flow of the business. Thus, movements on loans and provisions can be combined, while it is possible to disguise underlying cash flow by careful use of subtotals. This should be cleared up by the new accounting standard in the UK on cash flows. The format in table 2.5 concentrates on cash flows and aims to be almost brutal in identifying how the business is being funded.

Note that there is a deliberate split between short-term and long-term items. The purpose of this is to identify how much cash the business is generating or consuming from day-to-day activities. Many external lenders and investors in group situations will expect the trading cash flow to be able to fund new capital expenditure and dividend payments. If the trading cash flow is negative then this may point to an unsustainable business or one which is consuming too much cash in working capital (alternatively, this may be part of a deliberate business strategy for a growing business). This format will allow the treasurer to make pertinent comments to his or her colleagues about the cash flow of the business.

As with the receipts and payments method, the basic forecast can be prepared at business-unit level, therefore it may be useful to introduce lines for inter-company payments.

Different businesses will have different concepts of profit. It will be useful to try to express the true underlying level of profit by excluding non-recurring items such as profit on property sales and extraordinary and exceptional items.

Table 2.5 Format for source and application method

	Period 1	Period 2
+ Profit before tax		
+ Depreciation − Associates' profits +/− Other non-cash items − Profit on asset disposals		
− Increase/(decrease) in stock − Increase/(decrease) in debtors − Tax paid + Increase/(decrease) in creditors +/− Other short-term movements		
Trading cash flow		
+ Asset sales + Dividend receipts +/− Other long-term/non-recurring receipts + Receipts from associates		
− Capital expenditure − Dividend payments − New investment in associates		
Net movement		

Forecasting Liquidity

These frequently include non-cash elements which obviously do not form part of a cash forecast. For cash elements, it is better to show these separately in the bottom half of the forecast.

When calculating the movements in the components of working capital, careful separation of any unusual elements such as a debtor due an uncompleted property sale will allow a better understanding of what is actually going on as well as helping to calculate the business cash flow.

For all other elements, the need is to concentrate on the cash which is actually going to flow in the period under consideration. Virtually all of these items should be generated by a normal management accounts package.

Many of the points for special attention described in the preparation of a receipts and payments forecast still apply here – in particular the risk that large or irregular items are forgotten just because they do not form part of routine control.

Once each business unit's forecast has been prepared and these have been consolidated on a group basis, if necessary, then there is the need to add the following lines to take account of major capital flows:

- − debt repayments;
- − new deposits;
- + maturing deposits;
- + new debt receipts;
- + fresh equity receipts.

Notice that interest payments and receipts have not been mentioned explicitly. This is because their treatment depends on the particular style of internal management reporting.

If it is usual to show profit post-interest then there it is necessary to ensure that there have been correct adjustments in debtors and creditors. A safer treatment would be to show profit before both interest and tax and then show cash interest payments and receipts in the same manner as tax.

Using the two methods in combination

In the same way that the receipts and payments method is inappropriate for longer-term forecasts, the source and application method would be unwieldy for short-term forecasts and would also not allow an adequate level of control.

Depending upon the pressures within the business, the level of control and accuracy will vary. So, for example, a business experiencing severe liquidity problems would require very precise daily forecasts for perhaps the next 4 weeks, all prepared on a receipts and payments method. These would be followed by weekly forecasts for the following 2 months, again prepared by the same method. Then, a source and application method might be used for the following 3 months. If the liquidity problems were severe, going further could be an unnecessary diversion of management time.

However, in normal circumstances, a typical profile might be:

1 Receipts and payments:
   (a) daily for the next 3–5 days;
   (b) weekly for the following 3–12 weeks.
2 Then source and application:
   (a) monthly for the remainder of the year;
   (b) annually for the following 2–4 years.

Thus there would be a gradual build-up of a cash profile over the next 5 years.

Forecasting Liquidity

For months 4–6 there could be a blending of the methods, by paying particular attention to the underlying assumptions for working capital and by taking special care over large items.

When considering the forecasts for the next few months, however they have been prepared, it will be important to identify the peak borrowing requirement within a month. If forecasts are prepared on a month-end basis and the peak cash outflow occurs mid-month, a false sense of security might occur, especially for companies near to the limit of their borrowing facilities.

Problems in Groups

While the theory of forecasting cash extends to groups by consolidating individual subsidiaries or divisions, there are a number of practical points which may cause problems.

Even though the cash forecast may have been prepared by reliable colleagues in subsidiaries or other group functions, the treasurer should still examine the forecasts submitted for commercial sense and internal consistency. Errors can and do occur – what is important is the availability of reliable figures rather than apportioning blame.

Cash-book or cleared balance?

A cleared balance is the amount of cash in the bank which has passed through the clearing process (see chapter 5) and is available for use to receive interest or reduce interest charges. For short-term purposes, this is the figure that the treasurer should use for funding and investment decisions. The cash-book figure is the accountant's figure of cash and will include cheques banked and exclude cheques written. However, many of these cheques will not have completed the clearing cycle (indeed, some cheques may still be in the post to the suppliers) and so the bank's view of cash available (or overdrawn) is not the same as the accountant's view. In large groups, the difference may represent millions of pounds.

It is important, therefore, to issue clear instructions on how the forecast is to be prepared. In practice, it will be preferable to prepare forecasts for the next few days (and certainly for the close of the current day) on a cleared basis. Individual business units can provide details of cheques issued and make reasoned assumptions on the number of working days taken for cheques to clear through the system. Similarly, agreements will have been reached with banks on the clearing cycle for payments lodged and these can be factored into the forecast.

Longer-term forecasts can be supplied on a cash-book basis, particularly as this will be consistent with other business forecasts. The treasurer can then make a necessary group adjustment for interest forecasts.

In businesses with severe liquidity problems, minds will be particularly focused on the cleared position, but an eye will need to be kept on large cheques being specially presented.

Different assumptions

It usually goes without saying that clear instructions are given for preparation of all business forecasts in well-run groups. However, cash forecasts are prepared at different times and more frequently than profit forecasts. Therefore, the treasurer will need to review all forecasts for consistency. These include standard assumptions about interest and

Forecasting Liquidity

exchange rates, but most importantly about the timing of payments.

Intra-group payments are a particular problem, where disputes between subsidiaries can often mean that the paying unit will not forecast for political reasons. This does not help the treasurer and only clear and rigorous rules will solve the problem. It is always necessary to check that all intra-group payments match.

For particularly large items, such as the sale of a building, the cleared versus cash-book problem becomes particularly acute. The only practical solution is for the treasurer to ask for detailed information and then to act on it independently. Over time, a wider understanding will assist, but the risk of different assumptions will never be totally removed

Who prepares the forecast?

In spite of clear instructions, the treasurer does not have ultimate control of the preparation of the forecast in the subsidiary. Often a great deal of education may need to take place before forecasts are submitted to the required standard on a consistent basis. One particular risk arises from the use of the source and application method. One of the great advantages of this method is that it is *supposed* to tie in with the other business forecasts. This will be negated if the cash forecast is calculated by one person and submitted independently from the other forecasts. It is helpful, therefore, to insist that longer-term cash forecasts are submitted with profit forecasts, thus forcing the subsidiary finance director to focus on internal consistency. If this does not happen, there could be the embarrassing position of a substantial difference between the treasurer's view of the future cash position of the group and that of the financial controller!

Informal arrangements and group politics

The treasurer has a different function in a group from that of the controller or divisional finance director. A prime need for the treasurer is to understand exactly what will happen to the cash position on any given day – others may be more concerned with setting and meeting targets. Thus, it may not be uncommon for targets to be set and forecasts produced which the division knows cannot be met precisely. Thus, payments may actually be 2 or 3 days late, but it would be politically unacceptable to submit this forecast to the centre (or even to the divisional chief executive officer (CEO). Alternatively, a particular division may knowingly set optimistic targets for its own reasons.

The treasurer has to try to obtain all relevant information to establish the cash position as well as to determine the most likely outturn. Therefore, it may not be unusual for the treasurer to establish an informal network of contacts with the the divisions to ensure that there is a reliable flow of information. This network is likely to be the very people who are submitting the forecast. Naturally, the role of the treasurer extends to getting out into the divisions in order to understand their business, both to manage the liquidity of the group and also to represent the group effectively to the financial community. The operation of such an informal arrangement will be an art in itself and will bring the treasurer's interpersonal skills to the fore.

Obtaining the Opening Position

As with all forecasts, it is essential that we know where we are starting. The most accurate method of obtaining the opening position is to ask the bank. This may be done either by telephone or via an on-line balance reporting service (see chapter 5). It is likely to be supplied on a cleared basis, but will also provide useful information on payments due to clear during the current day. It is most unlikely that this will be the same as was forecast the previous day. A brief variance analysis will need to be carried out to ensure a better forecast for the day.

For longer-term forecasts, prepared on a cash-book basis, a reconciliation between cash and cleared will allow a better understanding of the forecast, although the cash-book opening position will be the figure which ultimately will be used.

Conclusion

Cash forecasts are important in the financial management of a business and are central to many decisions. However, the time spent on them and the detail of their preparation will be dictated by the size of organization. The techniques set out in this chapter can be used by businesses of all sizes, but the frequency of preparing and reviewing forecasts will depend upon the circumstances.

3
The Management of Uncertainty

> - How to begin to take decisions when real life does not turn out as originally forecast

Preparation of a cash forecast is all well and good, but it is not an end in itself – cash forecasts have to be used. In chapter 2, the main uses of cash forecasts were described. However, simply because a cash forecast has been prepared does not mean that, for example, the level of borrowings forecast would be the appropriate level of facilities to be arranged. Forecasts need interpretation.

More importantly, it would be startling if reality always matched the forecast position. Life may not turn out the way that has been expected, items may have been missed out, there may be forecasting bias or simply errors. Therefore, each forecast will need to be considered carefully from a number of viewpoints in order to decide what to do.

Checking against Past Forecasts

As with all forecasts, it is often instructive to compare reality with previous forecasts. This has a number of benefits:

The Management of Uncertainty

1. It looks for bias by the person preparing the forecast. The main use of a cash forecast is to establish the borrowing or investment requirements of the business and, as such, it is the absolute amount required or available that is important. So, if a particular individual takes a cautious view on sales, this may be compounded in a group situation if the treasurer takes the same view. If the existence of bias can be established, then the output of the forecast may be interpreted.
2. It helps to identify structural changes in the business. It may be, for example, that cash has followed a particular seasonal pattern in the past and that this has continued in recent forecasts. Any changes in a fast-moving business tend to be identified most quickly by changes in cash positions.
3. It will help to avoid illiquidity by looking for longer term errors and over-optimism in past forecasts. This type of analysis should also be carried out for associated accounting forecasts. Crucially, though, this focuses on the cash position.

A typical variance analysis could be represented graphically (figure 3.1).

Seasonal PLC has prepared forecasts over a number of periods (table 3.1). Thus, in period 0, the forecast for two periods ahead was (84), this was revised to (85) in period 1 and actually turned out to be (90). In this case forecasts have been consistently over-optimistic, representing a belief that sales will eventually recover – we will return to this case in chapter 8.

This type of analysis should clearly show any of the trends described above. Any forecast should be expected to vary from the actual result within a realistic margin. This may represent a percentage of sales or receipts. Naturally any significant variance should be investigated. If bias within a division is the cause, it may be more politic in the first instance to recognize the bias and to compensate for it. In the

Table 3.1 Seasonal PLC: cash forecasts (£m)

| | \multicolumn{6}{c}{Forecasts prepared in period} |
Date	0	1	2	3	4	5
0	8A					
1	(22)	(24)A				
2	(84)	(85)	(90)A			
3	(90)	(93)	(100)	(110)A		
4	(15)	(20)	(25)	(40)	(50)A	
5	73	75	60	50	20	
6	143	140	120	110	80	
7		140	110	90	80	
8			60	50	25	
9				0	(15)	

A = actual.

long term, however, such a bias will need to be removed, and control procedures instated to try to avoid biases and errors in the future.

Once a particular team of people has been preparing forecasts for some time, familiarity will lead to an intuitive understanding of the likely outcome and the action required. However, consistent and high quality reporting must be maintained to avoid complacency.

Trends or detail

A question which frequently arises is whether to look at detailed variances or just to consider the trends. In some ways this is related to the time-scales involved.

The Management of Uncertainty

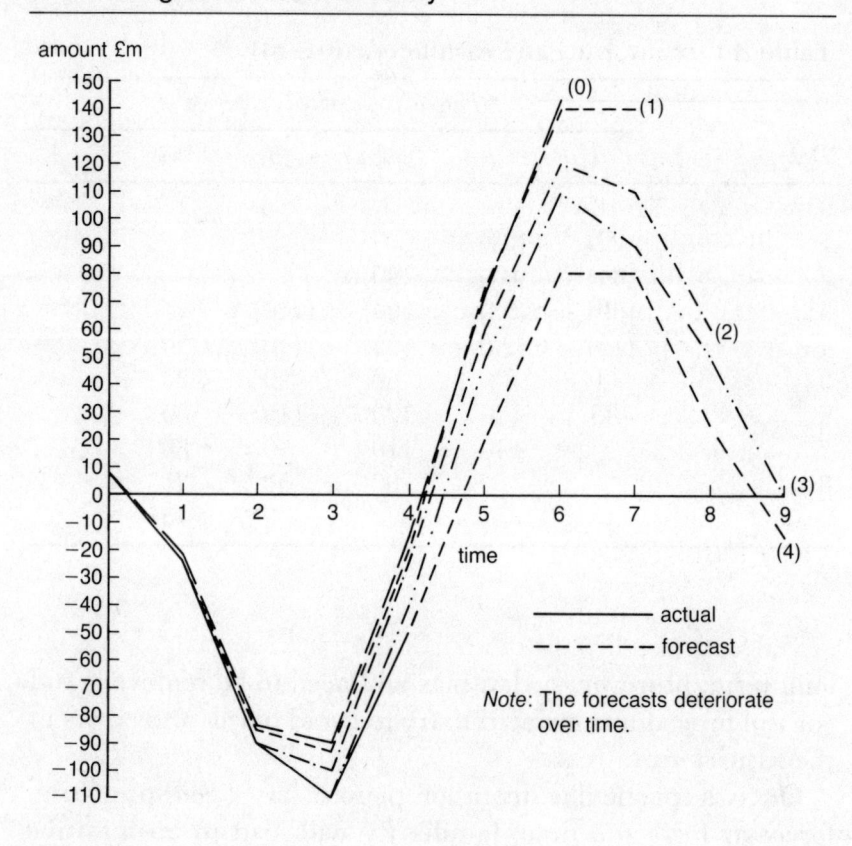

Figure 3.1 A typical variance analysis

Frequently, variances to forecast are explained by very cogent reasoning, such as this sale did not arise or that happened late. However, if trends are looked at, these may show a consistent pattern – the management issues which generally arise from such a realization are beyond the scope of this book – but the treasurer will be able to recognize the consequences and act accordingly.

In the short term, however, detailed examination is important as this will show more detailed errors in reasoning. Also, it might point out any compensating issues which could arise – such as receipt from a delayed sale. Alternatively, a cash forecast might only have been achieved by delaying payments to creditors – these will have to be met at some stage.

The condition of the business will also direct the emphasis. Clearly, a business in a liquidity crisis will need to consider the detail. A more secure business will be able to concentrate on trends – however, the detailed examination will need to be prepared by someone, but possibly more as part of a control process.

How Much?

Even with the benefit of analysis of past forecasts, life is still unlikely to turn out the way expected. This will not be a fault of the forecasting techniques, but because business assumptions vary from reality.

So, what could be different?

- changes in the economic environment;
- cancellation of a major contract;
- success in an unexpected contract;
- an unexpected acquisition is made;
- an unexpected disposal is made;
- forecasting errors in business assumptions;
- the board changes its mind.

And, on a smaller scale:

- increase in bad debts;
- pressure from creditors to accelerate payments;
- lack of stock control leading to increased cash.

The Management of Uncertainty

The central issue is how to use the cash forecast despite the effect of all these variables.

The key requirement of liquidity management is to ensure that there is enough cash to meet liabilities as they fall due. Therefore, for all relevant time horizons, the treasurer will need to look critically at the cash forecast and consider how reality might vary in order to establish how liquidity requirements could be met. These might be achieved by maintaining large cash balances or by arranging the necessary level of borrowing facilities or by a mixture of the two. There will be a trade-off of cost against the returns the business can generate. On a short time-scale, consider the following situation.

Company A

The cash forecast for Company A shows that the bank position on a cleared basis tonight will be £500,000 in credit and that the company has an overdraft facility of £250,000. It is not in the interest of the business to leave credit balances on a current account not earning interest. Therefore, the normal procedure would be to deposit perhaps £600,000 to give an overdrawn balance of £100,000. However, if past analysis shows that there could be errors of as much as £200,000 in cash forecasts, then this would leave Company A exposed to a breach its overdraft facility with all the attendant consequences. This is a far greater treasury sin than leaving a credit balance not earning interest.

Therefore, in this instance, a lower deposit of £500,000 would be placed (assuming no other major variables) and the risk would be run of a credit balance of £200,000 (arising from an error of £200,000). Finally, assuming that this business has a reasonable credit standing, a higher overdraft facility should be negotiated.

The Management of Uncertainty

For medium- and longer-term issues, the procedure becomes more complex. The overriding need is to ensure that liquidity will be available when required. There are other sources of liquidity than accessible bank balances; others include:

- investments with a ready market, such as bank certificates of deposit;
- undrawn *committed* borrowing facilities;
- debtors that may be factored;
- assets with a liquid market.

The specific features of these instruments and markets will be explained in chapter 6, but what is important for the purposes of this chapter is that their potential availability is recognized. Consider the two simple examples below.

Company B

Company B has £10 million available to deposit for 6 months; however, there is a 50% chance that £5 million will be required for an acquisition in 3 months' time. Interest rates currently favour longer deposit periods.

The specific questions of managing the interest rate problem will be considered in chapters 4 and 7, but for the purposes of liquidity, the likely need for cash is significant. If further borrowing facilities are not available, then there are two options that need to be considered:

1. Either deposit £5 million for 6 months and the other £5 million for 3 months and see what life is like then. Or

The Management of Uncertainty

2 Invest £5,000,000 in a liquid investment for 6 months, recognizing that there may be a capital loss in 3 months if it has to be sold.

Company C

Company C has prepared a cash forecast for the next year which shows that it will only just manage with its available borrowing facilities. The treasurer also believes that there is a risk that sales will begin to turn down. In short, the business risk is high.

The problem here is more general than just selecting an interest period and it would appear that the usual option of negotiating sufficient backstop facilities is not possible. In this instance, there are a number of good business practices which should be implemented to avoid illiquidity:

- frequent forecasts to recognize problems early;
- review the management of working capital;
- prepare to sell certain assets ahead of problems;
- review the potential to factor debtors;
- attempt to reduce stocks;
- attempt to obtain additional trade credit without risking supplier goodwill;
- consider raising equity.

Naturally, real life is going to be more complicated than these examples, both because there will be other issues to be considered and because decisions are seldom this clear-cut. However, there are general principles to be applied in the management of uncertainty. The most important of these is the ability to recognize what might happen and develop strategies to deal with the possible as well as the probable.

The Management of Uncertainty

The more complex issues of managing uncertainty and liquidity will be re-examined in chapter 9, while the intervening chapters will look at interest rate management, the use of bank systems and the various markets involved.

4
The Structure of Interest Rates and the Yield Curve

- The methods of quoting interest rates
- How to interpret what a particular interest rate means

Once we have established how much cash there is available to deposit or is needed to be borrowed, we can consider time scales and the level of return we require. For the purposes of this chapter, let us assume that all possible investments are of equal risk so that the prime consideration is the absolute level of return.

The cash flow forecast will have indicated the length of time for which cash is available or required, but there are a wide range of decisions that can be taken in that period. Before exploring these, it is necessary to understand something about the structure of interest rates.

People are generally familiar with the concept that interest rates change all the time in the present world, but the personal experience tends to be limited to those occasions when there is a major shift brought about by a change in mortgage rates or savings-account rates. These changes are relatively infrequent, more because of the costs of notifying changes and the associated marketing costs than because in

Interest Rates and the Yield Curve

the wholesale money-markets changes occur almost every minute. This is the essential feature of a *floating interest rate*.

Another general feature of the personal situation is that interest is not usually credited or charged on a daily basis, but at the end of a given period (say annually) no matter what has happened to interest rates in the meantime.

In the wholesale markets, interest rates are usually quoted at a set rate for a given period, with interest paid at the end of that period. Thus, a rate might be quoted as

1 month 11.5% p.a.

This means that, if we are talking about surplus funds, then for a deposit lasting 1 month, interest will be paid at the annual rate of 11.5% and the interest and principal will be repaid at the end of that month. Interest is calculated by using the actual number of days involved and assuming that a year has 365 days for sterling and 360 days for most other currencies.

Hence, in this example if the deposit were £1 million and the exact number of days was 31, then the total interest would be

$$1,000,000 \times 11.5/100 \times 31/365 = £9767.12$$

But if the deposit was $1,000,000, then the interest calculation would be

$$1,000,000 \times 11.5/100 \times 31/360 = \$9902.78$$

Bid and Offer

Naturally, the same rates are not quoted for both deposits and borrowing. If a bank is looking for deposits then it will *bid* for

Interest Rates and the Yield Curve

those deposits, if it is looking to lend to another bank (that is, place a deposit with another bank), then it will *offer*: this gives rise to the concept of bid and offer rates. These might be quoted as follows:

Overnight	$11\frac{1}{8}$–11
7 days	$11\frac{1}{16}$–11
1 month	11–$10\frac{1}{2}$
3 months	$10\frac{7}{8}$–$10\frac{3}{4}$
6 months	$10\frac{11}{16}$–$10\frac{5}{8}$

(Note that these are all per annum rates.) Thus a bank will agree to take deposits at $10\frac{3}{4}$% p.a. for 3 months fixed, or will lend (to other banks) at $11\frac{1}{16}$% p.a. for 7 days.

LIBOR and Basis Points

The rates that are quoted above represent the rates at which prime banks would be prepared to deal with each other. For other weaker banks or for companies, rates will tend to be higher then the offer rate. Equally, since prime banks tend to be strong and can therefore attract deposits more easily, they tend to have lower bid rates.

The offer rate used by major international banks is known as **LIBOR** (the London inter-bank offered rate), i.e. the rate at which a bank is prepared to place a deposit with a prime bank. The LIBOR tends to be the bench-mark rate for wholesale money-market dealings. There will be a different LIBOR for different currencies and also each bank will set its own LIBOR.

There are also related rates: LIBID represents the rate at which a bank is willing to accept a deposit and LIMEAN is the average of a given pair of LIBID and LIBOR.

Interest Rates and the Yield Curve

There are also rates used, based on financial centres other than London, such as PIBOR for Paris, FIBOR for Frankfurt. These are particularly relevant for local currencies, but the use of modern technology should mean that rates converge very quickly.

Interest on loans is often quoted over LIBOR – for banks this represents their profit margin as well as the costs of complying with the capital adequacy requirements of the Bank of England and other central banks. The margin over LIBOR may be expressed as so many percentage points, e.g. $\frac{1}{2}$% p.a. or it may be expressed as a given number of basis points. A *basis point* is $\frac{1}{100}$% p.a., so $\frac{1}{2}$% is the same as 50 basis points. This terminology has become more popular as banks have moved away from quoting in $\frac{1}{16}$ths and $\frac{1}{8}$ths and now use 5 or 10 basis points (or, of course any number, usually much higher!)

Selecting an Interest Period

If there is a sum available for deposit for 6 months and the rates above are quoted, how can an interest period be chosen? One obvious alternative is to deposit for 6 months at $10\frac{5}{8}$% p.a. But a different choice might be to deposit for 3 months at $10\frac{3}{4}$% and then redeposit at the end of 3 months. The real problem is that we do not know what interest rates are going to be in 3 months' time. Naturally, we can form our own judgement but we can also look at what the market expects to happen to interest rates.

The Yield Curve

If the interest rates for given periods are plotted on a graph against time then this will give a curve, known as the yield curve. A yield curve can be for any period, lasting up to say 20 years.

The basic shape of the yield curve will tell us in general terms what the market is expecting to happen to interest rates. There are three typical shapes of the yield curve: normal or upward, flat and inverse.

Normal or upward

In this case, rates are progressively higher for longer periods (figure 4.1). In a stable interest rate environment this should occur naturally for three reasons:

1. *The effect of compound interest.* If we deposited for 3 months, collected the interest and redeposited for 3 months at the same rate, we would end up with a greater amount than if we had just deposited at that rate for 6 months at the outset.

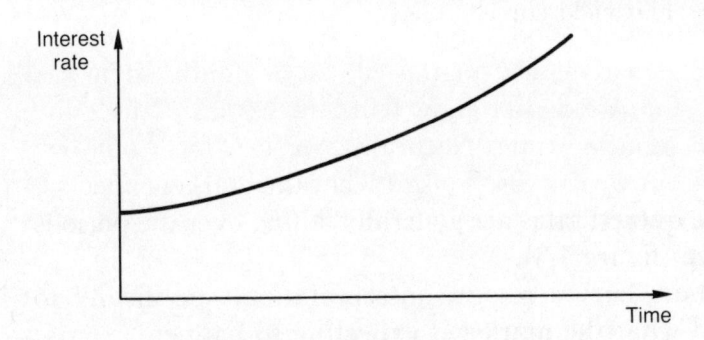

Figure 4.1 Normal yield curve

Interest Rates and the Yield Curve

2 *Liquidity preference*. If we are offered the same effective return over two different periods, then all other things being equal, we would choose the shorter period as it provides greater flexibility.
3 *Credit risk*. The longer the period of investment, the greater the chance of default. This is clearly a more significant factor over the very long term.

Flat

In this case, the interest rates quoted are broadly the same over all periods being considered (figure 4.2).

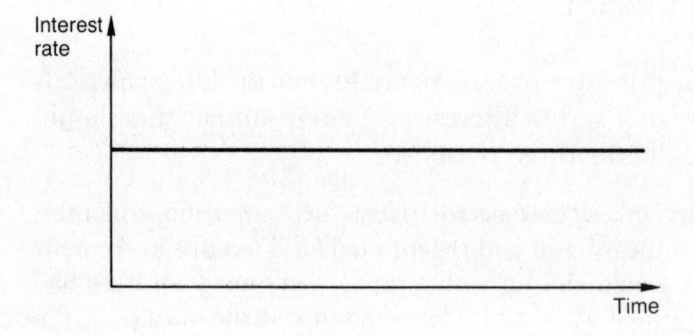

Figure 4.2 Flat yield curve

Inverse

In this case quoted rates are generally falling over the periods of the curve (figure 4.3).

All of these curves require interpretation, specifically to understand what the market is expecting to happen.

Interest Rates and the Yield Curve

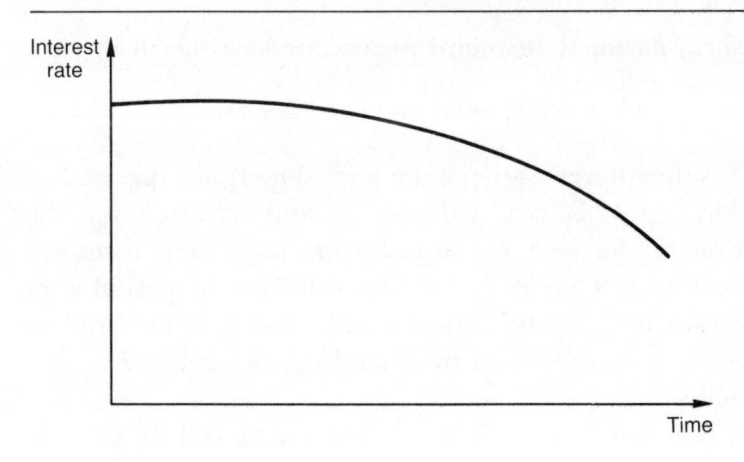

Figure 4.3 Inverse yield curve

Disaggregation

If we are quoted 12% for a 3 month investment and also 12% for a 6 month investment then all other things being equal it would be logical to choose to invest for 3 months and then reinvest in 3 months to gain the benefits of compounding. If this were the situation, one could deduce that the market anticipates that rates will be lower for 3 months in 3 months' time, otherwise everybody would be making money this way.

By removing the effects of compounding or disaggregating then we can calculate what the market expects rates to be for 3 months in 3 months' time. Assuming equal whole months, the interest for 3 months and 6 months respectively on £1 million at 12% is £30,000 and £60,000.

So what rate would produce £30,000 for the second 3 months on a deposit of £1,030,000? The answer is 11.65%, i.e. the market expects the 3-month rate in 3 months' time to be 11.65%.

Interest Rates and the Yield Curve

The formula for the general case is:

$$(1 + im)(1 + in) = (1 + i(m+n))$$

where: i is the interest rate p.a. for a given period expressed as a fraction (so 12% p.a. will be $\frac{12}{100}$) and adjusted for the proportion of the year (so a 12% p.a. rate for a 6 month period will be $\frac{12}{100} \times \frac{6}{12}$), im the interest rate i for the period m, in the interest rate i for the period n and $i(m+n)$ is the interest rate i for the period formed by extending the period m by the period n.

So, in the above case m is 3, n is 3 and $m+n$ is 6. If we were to calculate the 12% example this way, it would be

$$(1 + 0.12 \times 3/12) \times (1 + x \times 3/12) = (1 + 0.12 \times 6/12)$$

or

$$1.03 \times (1 + x \times 3/12) = 1.06$$

so

$$x = (1.06/1.03 - 1) \times 12/3$$
$$= 0.1165$$

or

$$11.65\% \text{ p.a.}$$

Using the rates given above in the section on bid and offer in this chapter we can calculate what the market expects 3 month rates to be in 3 months' time in the same way. Thus:

$$(1 + 0.1075 \times 3/12) \times (1 + x \times 3/12) = (1 + 0.10625 \times 6/12)$$

or

$$1.026875 \times (1 + x/4) = 1.053125$$

so

$$x = 0.102252$$

or

10.2252% p.a.

Interpreting the Yield Curve

From the example of 12% for both 3 and 6 months, we can deduce that a flat yield curve means that the market expects interest rates to fall over time. Consequently, an inverse yield curve means that interest rates are expected to fall more sharply over the period.

In the case of a normal yield curve, the degree of the slope becomes important. If the slope is very gentle, interest rates may still be expected to fall, but a steeper slope might mean that market expectations are for interest rates to remain broadly stable and steeper slopes still to increase.

The general understanding of the shape of the yield curve lets the treasurer make broad decisions on the period of investment or borrowing to be selected. But first the treasurer will need to have his or her own view on interest rates. Thus, presented with a flat yield curve but the belief that interest rates will rise, an investor will select a short period, anticipating an increase in rates.

The *efficient market hypothesis* would imply that the treasurer should have no reason to believe that rates should be any different from those implied by the yield curve and that the period to be selected should match the period for which funds are available or required. In practice, there are a number of reasons why this does not take place. First, people will take

Interest Rates and the Yield Curve

different views and this is especially so in particularly volatile markets. There may be more liquidity in the more common periods of 3 or 6 months which could provide times where rates do not match precisely those expected by the market for other interest periods. More commonly, however, it is by no means clear for how long the funds are available or required, or indeed it may be for such a long period that consecutive shorter periods have to be chosen. Given this situation, there is a need to take active decisions on interest periods, and the combination of the yield curve and the treasurer's own view of interest rates will form the major basis for the decision (along with amount and the actual period of surplus or requirement).

Risk

One major situation where the anticipation of rising or falling rates is not the dominant factor is when a company (or an individual, for that matter) cannot afford the consequences of rates rising or falling below a particular level. This might be because the additional interest cost (in the case of a borrower) could not be serviced and the company forced into liquidation. Alternatively, a company which derives a high proportion of its profit from interest income might be unwilling to risk a reduction in profit. This might mean that whatever the treasurer's own views on interest rates, a safe policy may need to be adopted by choosing longer periods to secure particular interest rates. This question will be examined in greater depth in chapter 7.

Above all, a regular examination of the implications of the yield curve should alert the treasurer to the degree of interest rate risk.

Annualized Percentage Rates (APRs) and Absolute Return

Naturally, in spite of the discussion of the alternative rates available, it is the absolute level of return or cost which becomes important (assuming a consistent exposure to credit risk).

Another factor to be evaluated in the selection of interest periods is the comparison of the returns available from different maturities. Thus, how can we compare 10.5%p.a. with interest paid quarterly with 11% p.a. with interest paid annually? The basic method is to put them on to a common basis of the total return (or cost) over a full year. The use of a year also matches most company reporting periods and thus will be the measure most familiar to other colleagues.

In the case of 10.5% with interest quarterly, the total return is going to be

$$\left(1 + \frac{0.105}{4}\right)^4 = 1.1092$$

i.e. the total return (or APR) is 10.92%. This means that on an investment of £1 million, the total return would be approximately £109,200. This can be confirmed:

Interest at end of first quarter = £26,250
Interest on £1,026,250 at end of second quarter = £26,939
Interest on £1,053,189 at end of third quarter = £27,646
Interest on £1,080,835 at end of fourth quarter = £28,371

i.e. a total return of £109,206. This would be compared with an APR of 11% in the case of annual interest and, assuming constant expectations of interest rates, the return from 11% would be higher. As with the interpretation of the yield curve,

Interest Rates and the Yield Curve

this can be but part of the information on which to base a decision.

Note that the general formula for the APR of an instrument with nominal interest rate of r (quoted as r% p.a.), but with interest paid after d days on the basis of a 365-day year (see above) is

$$\left(1 + \frac{rd}{36{,}500}\right)^{365/d}$$

The answer will be quoted as $1.x$ where x is the resultant APR. Naturally this formula assumes that reinvestment will be available at the same rate at the end of d days, but that is all part of the central problem.

In order to give a general feel, table 4.1 lists various APRs with the compared quoted rates. So, it is useful to note that approximately 11.5% p.a. quoted for a 3 month rate will give a total return of 12% p.a. (Note: the definition of APR in the UK for consumer credit is defined precisely by law and this definition should not be confused with the discussion here – although both aim at the same idea.)

Table 4.1 Various APRs compared with quoted rates

Months	APR(%) 9	10	11	12	15
1	8.65	9.57	10.48	11.39	14.06
2	8.68	9.61	10.53	11.44	14.14
3	8.71	9.65	10.57	11.49	14.22
6	8.81	9.77	10.71	11.66	14.48
12	9.00	10.00	11.00	12.00	15.00

Performance Measurement

Performance measurement is one of the great unsolved questions in treasury management. However, targets often need to be set to satisfy the profitability requirement. Targets cannot be absolute, as they need to have restrictions on credit and risk established, but once these are accounted for then targets such as the daily average over a given period of 1 or 3 month LIBID (or another chosen average such as 1 *and* 3 month LIBID) may be suitable.

5
Managing your Bank and Bank Services

- How a banker-customer relationship should be arranged
- Money transmission and electronic banking products.

The banking system is critical to the efficient management of liquidity for all businesses. In addition to the borrowing and depositing services described in chapter 6 and the hedging products described in chapter 7, the day-to-day operation of bank accounts and money transmission are essential to the smooth running of a business. In this chapter, we shall look at some of the money transmission and other products which banks offer and which are involved in liquidity management.

Managing your Banker

But first, it is helpful to look at how the banker-customer relationship should operate. There have been many complaints over the past few years about how banks have treated their customers, particularly small businesses. On the other hand, many banks have complained about a trend to transaction, rather than relationship banking by large companies.

Managing your Bank and Bank Services

Transaction banking involves taking each item of business to whoever offers the keenest price, while relationship banking involves a certain amount of give and take on the final element of pricing, in return for consistent service.

In approaching its banker, the business needs to know what its requirements are going to be. It also needs to have decided what its ethic of operation is going to be – relationship or just driven by price. Banks are businesses themselves and need to make a return as well as ensure that bad debts do not arise; however, they are also sensitive to competition on price which might drive away good business. As much as any business would want to ensure the continuing supply at the right quality of an essential raw material and would, therefore, recognize short-term price-cutting, then so it should regard its bank as a supplier – of money and related products.

The first stage for the business, of whatever size, is to gain the confidence of its banker – especially if borrowing is going to be involved. Banks make an assessment of the character of the management of a business a very substantial part of any credit judgement. This will often be best achieved by being able to make a clear presentation about the business – what it does and what is anticipated for the future. There should also be a clear explanation of who does what in the management team – banks are just as interested in the non-financial management as well as in the more direct contacts.

If borrowing is to be sought, then there should be a clear financial presentation available. This should not just concentrate on profit and loss and balance sheet – important though these are – there will need to be a clear cash flow forecast, rather in the form shown in chapter 2. There should be a monthly projection for the following few months, followed by quarterly or yearly projections for the next few years. (Very large businesses may not be required to go through this detailed presentation, as a track record will have been established.) This should demonstrate the ability to repay or refinance borrowings. The projections should show how the loan is to be serviced and repaid. The prospective borrower will also need to be ready to discuss the sensitivities of the business. The bank will want to satisfy itself that the cash flow and the profit projections are consistent with each other – so there will be no point in trying to dress the figures as a good banker should be able to see what is going on.

The trust and understanding which should be established at this stage will allow both a more understanding approach to be taken at any time when there are difficulties, but may also result in more beneficial charges in the light of a consistent business relationship. There are a number of intangible benefits which result from a secure understanding with one's banker; these include:

- The banker will be more prepared to spend time understanding your business problems.
- The bank will be able to identify products which are suitable for the business.
- The banker is more likely to push credit applications to his or her superiors and with more personal commitment.
- Errors (which will inevitably occur) can be sorted out quickly.
- The general level of service should be better.

Of course, these are natural human reactions when anyone takes the time to understand another person, but if banks are approached on the basis of business partners rather than adversaries, then there is more chance of making good progress.

Bank Products for Liquidity

The products which are described below generally need customizing to the particular circumstances. In order to make them most effective, there will have to be a detailed understanding between the appropriate clerical staff in the bank and their opposite numbers in the company.

Money transmission

The business of moving money around, for whatever reason, is a significant issue for business. As companies trade internationally, the logistics become complicated and the cost and amounts involved mean that the potential for loss increases. Money transmission is at the heart of modern banking and banks have invested in systems to manage the process efficiently. Companies can often benefit significantly by devoting time to organizing carefully the process of paying and receiving funds. If there is a significant volume involved, putting this business out to tender can result in lower costs, as well as different ideas from different banks on how it can be organized. However, banks frequently find this type of business attractive as it involves income without a lending risk, therefore it should normally be offered for tender to those domestic banks which provide the full range of money transmission services. Equally, for those companies with limited borrowing facilities, it is often helpful to couple the granting of the tender for money transmission with the requirement to provide an appropriate level of borrowing facilities. The worst of all worlds would be to withdraw the money transmission business from one bank, for it only to withdraw a lending facility without a replacement facility in place.

However, no amount of hard negotiation will compensate for poor administration within the company. In particular, the cost of interest for many businesses means that all receipts should be paid into the bank *as soon as possible*. Many businesses incur significant hidden costs because cheques have to be kept in some form of administration department for reconciliation before they are paid in. This represents a large hidden cost, as well as exposing the business to higher bad debts due to bouncing cheques or to customers changing their minds.

Cheques

Cheques are familiar as a method of payment, but there are important differences from the personal situation. The most notable of these are charges and the clearance cycle. Banks charge their business customers both for cheques issued and for cheques paid into the business account. These are a matter for negotiation and will depend, in particular, on the volume involved. There are often alternatives to automate payments, thus removing the paper involved and providing an opportunity to negotiate lower charges. Banks sometimes charge as a percentage of turnover; however, it is often desirable to have charges based on the number of cheques involved, rather than be charged as a percentage of turnover. As the business grows, this gives greater scope to control costs.

If there are a significant number of cheques paid in (or if the typical value of each cheque is high), then there should be a clear understanding on when good value can be obtained. This represents not only the date at which funds are available for use, but also the date on which the cleared balance is

Managing your Bank and Bank Services

calculated for interest purposes. Most businesses should typically obtain 2 or 3 working day cycles. However, longer value dating may result in lower charges – although this trade-off should be transparent and will be unattractive for many small businesses trading near the limit of their borrowing facilities.

Cash

Most businesses only require cash facilities for petty cash purposes, which is not frequently a significant amount. However, for retailers and others dealing directly with the public, there is often a need to pay in substantial amounts of cash, as well as draw out cash in different denominations of note and coin. (It should be noted that smaller banks, building societies and the Post Office are substantial users of cash in the form of notes and coin.)

Although cash does not have quite the same bad debt possibilities as cheques, it does have very substantial costs of collection in the form of insurance, security and bank charges. These can make it more expensive to collect than cheques or credit cards. Companies will negotiate charges for the banking of cash with their business customers (it is far from free) and also clearing cycles in the same way as for cheques. Particular care needs to be taken on the terms agreed with the bank for handling cash. The trade off between the charge for handling cash and the number of days until value is obtained tends to be much more of a trade-off than for cheques, so it is not unusual to receive a higher quote for next-day value and a lower one for 2- or 3-day value.

For larger businesses, particularly competitive quotes can be obtained if the cash can be delivered in bulk to the bank's bullion centre. Each bank has a number of these around the country and the cash is delivered directly by the company's security carrier. The calculation of the most effective frequency for banking cash and the various costs involved is often complicated and frequently warrants the full-time attention of one individual for some weeks to calculate the optimum arrangements.

Credit and debit cards

These are processed in much the same way as cheques and there is a healthy market now for the major credit cards in the UK, although not for charge cards, where companies find some charges unacceptably high. It is a matter of judgement for each business to decide whether the incremental sales are genuinely additional sales (rather than substituting other methods of payment) and, therefore, worth the cost. Again, value dating is an important factor to negotiate, as well the charges and commissions involved.

Telegraphic transfers

If large sums have to be sent or received (especially internationally), then a telegraphic transfer (TT) is worth considering. This is a method where the funds are transferred electronically with same-day value for domestic payments from the paying business account directly to the receiving account. In order for this to occur, there first has to be an agreement between the payer and receiver concerned that payment will be made this way. The payer will often require some inducement to use this method of payment, as a cheque would doubtless be slower and cheaper.

In general, a break-even analysis will need to be calculated in order to establish whether or not a TT is worthwhile. If the incremental cost of using a TT is c and the number of days'

Managing your Bank and Bank Services

interest gained is d, with an interest rate of $i\%$ p.a., then the break-even amount for switching to a TT is

$$\frac{c \times 36{,}500}{i \times d}$$

So, if interest rates are 10% p.a. and the extra cost involved is £15 in order to gain 3 days' interest, then it is worth switching to a TT for all amounts greater than

$$\frac{15 \times 36{,}500}{10 \times 3} \text{ i.e £18,250}$$

For companies within the same group, TTs are the normal form of payment, but for trading partners there will need to be some commercial agreement to use TTs. For some industries, this may represent normal terms, for others a separate negotiation may be required.

In order for TTs to be effective, precise instructions will be needed of the bank and account to which the funds are to be transferred. The recipient should also have an arrangement to be notified when funds are received for large amounts so that they can be put to immediate use.

For international funds transfer, the added complication of different currencies means that the instructions have to be particularly clear and also, if accounts are not held in the relevant currency, it must be clear how the funds are to be obtained or applied. A particular risk here is that if no clear currency instructions have been given, then a significant proportion of the total amount will be absorbed in fairly expensive foreign exchange transactions.

There are variety of systems that are used by banks to make the payments involved. In the UK, the most usual system used for making same-day payments over £5000 is CHAPS (clearing house automated payments system). Large businesses may have a CHAPS terminal of their own which is

Managing your Bank and Bank Services

connected via a modem to their clearing bank's own system. If this type of system is to be used there need to be clear and tight controls on access to the system. Once payments have been released to the system they cannot be reversed. A particular way of exercising control is to insist that the system is set up so that payments can only be made to certain pre-set beneficiaries (say, other group companies or particular banks for their own account).

The most common system within the UK for payments that have to be made frequently, say payroll or to regular suppliers, is BACS (bankers automated clearing system). Companies supply details of the payments to be made on a pre-formatted magnetic tape which is then supplied to their bank. Payments need to be supplied a pre-set period in advance (usually two business days) and once they have been released into the system they cannot be cancelled and payment is guaranteed by the payer's bank. The automation of these payments can often result in substantially lower bank charges. The cost of BACS tends to be only a few pence per item whereas TTs cost pounds (overseas it is sometimes a percentage of the value involved without limit – care should be taken to ensure that a limit is in place otherwise simple transfers may cost thousands of pounds).

In addition, BACS can be used for the efficient collection of funds via the use of direct debits. This is common for public utilities and leasing companies, but it can have a wider application for collecting from general commercial customers. However, from the customer's point of view, it may not wish to give the control implied to its supplier.

International trade

In addition to the basic issue of transferring funds internationally, trading overseas has the added problems of more

Managing your Bank and Bank Services

complicated credit risk as well as political risk and cultural differences. The credit and political risk are often avoided by a mixture of using confirmed letters of credit, documentary collections and export insurance. These are complex areas which require detailed advice. However, exporters and importers need to understand how the various facilities operate and that the various risks involved can be removed (if they cannot, then there have to be very good reasons for the transaction involved).

Organizing Group Bank Accounts

The benefits of grouping together the bank accounts for different companies within the same group arises from economies of scale. These are both in terms of bank charges and overall interest costs. If, say, two companies are under common ownership and one is borrowing and one has surplus funds, then it is clearly beneficial to try to arrange matters so that interest is only charged on the net borrowed position or that the net surplus is invested most efficiently.

Banks will generally agree to charge interest on this basis (subject to certain safeguards described below) and there are two basic methods of arranging the bank accounts. Banks are now also able to provide reports apportioning interest between group companies; an example is given in table 5.1.

Netting

In this instance, each company maintains the balance on its own account and interest is only charged on the net overdrawn position (there tends not to be interest on credit

Managing your Bank and Bank Services

Table 5.1 National Westminster Bank PLC
Interest apportionment service. Interest apportionment for the period from 1 April to 30 April. Group name: XYZ PLC Group. IAS Reference: 0013/000 1

Sort code	Account number		Notional net interest	Notional debit interest received	Notional credit interest paid
60 30 06	01497243	Treasury account	0.00	0.00	0.00
60 30 06	01497189	Parent company	1297.71	1573.35	275.64-
01 10 01	86571133	Subsidiary company No 1	475.40-	465.25	939.65-
50 41 29	36486167	Subsidiary company No 2	228.40	345.77	117.37-
		Totals	1050.71	2383.37	1332.66-

Notional net interest:	1050.71
Less group overdraft interest:	634.89-
Treasury position:	415.82

Interest formulae debit rate 2.0000% above base rate.
Base rate from 1 April to 30 April   13,0000%.
Created on 2 May Time; 0855.

balances – see chapter 6 in the section on overdrafts). Interest may be charged to one central account or allocated on a basis specified by the company. It is often helpful, both for taxation and for cultural reasons, to arrange affairs so that interest is charged and credited at the same rate to all group companies, with the net effect that the whole group has only been charged on the net position.

The net position is calculated for all group accounts held with a particular branch, irrespective of branch. The central treasury department will hold a central account which is the one which will be used to arrange the desired net position.

Table 5.2 is an example of a netting system. In this example, the treasury department would transfer more than

Managing your Bank and Bank Services

Table 5.2 A netting system

	Forecast closing balance (£)	
Subsidiary A account	500,000	Dr
Subsidiary B account	950,000	Cr
Subsidiary C account	150,000	Cr
Net total	600,000	Cr

£600,000 from its central account and place it on deposit or use the funds elsewhere, so that net interest would be charged on the (hopefully small) net overdrawn position. In this case, the balances on subsidiaries B and C have been used to offset the costs for A for the group overall.

In addition to the scale economy benefits, there is also the benefit that the individual companies are allowed to continue to operate their own bank accounts, but are relieved of day-to-day treasury management. Therefore, this system works well in decentralized groups where operational management is given a high level of autonomy. It also allows clear control if cash targets have been set company by company.

Zero-balancing

In a netting system, no actual funds move between accounts, but there is an alternative method where funds are moved automatically at the end of each day so that all but one account has a zero balance. In the example above, zero-balancing would work as shown in table 5.3. The same amount of funds is available to the treasury as for netting system, but funds actually move.

Table 5.3 Zero-balancing

	Forecast closing balance (£)		Transfer in/(out) (£)
Subsidiary A account	500,000	Dr	500,000
Subsidiary B account	950,000	Cr	(950,000)
Subsidiary C account	150,000	Cr	(150,000)
Net transfer to treasury account			600,000

The choice of system depends upon the culture of the company involved. Zero-balancing implies a high degree of centralization, but it also means that it can be more difficult for individual subsidiaries to track their own cash flow. There is also a widely held view that the introduction of a netting system within a group assists cash forecasting.

Bank agreements

If zero-balancing is to be used then written instructions will have to be given to the bank and signed on behalf of each subsidiary involved.

In netting systems, each subsidiary will be allocated a separate overdraft limit and there will be a net overdraft limit for the group. If each subsidiary is creditworthy then this might be say £20 million for each subsidiary, but only £5 million for the group overall – this will allow greater flexibility in day-to-day management. If particular subsidiaries are less creditworthy, then a guarantee or letter of comfort may be taken – this avoids the risk that all the borrowing ends up in the weakest company.

The bank may take a letter of set-off from all the companies involved, but increasingly full cross-guarantees from all companies involved are taken. This will allow it to set off credit and debit balances without notice. This provision is only likely to be used in insolvency, but it does allow the bank to use its own capital base effectively and therefore offer higher overdraft limits to individual subsidiaries. Care should be taken that the set-off arrangement is approved by the board of each subsidiary, otherwise directors who were not party to the agreement might be able to sue those who did sign the agreement in the event that insolvency occurs and funds are transferred out of that particular subsidiary.

Balance Reporting Systems

One of the central problems in cash management is obtaining enough information to make good decisions. The advances in technology now allow banks to provide PC-based balance reporting systems. These allow companies access to both the nominal and cleared position on their bank accounts directly in their own offices. The use of a PC avoids manual intervention, allowing management to begin as early as desired and also reduces the possibility of error. A typical example might be shown in table 5.4.

Details may often be pooled from different banks so that complete reports can be obtained and integrated into group reporting. The use of satellites and other communications networks can provide detailed reports world-wide in different currencies (table 5.5). This level of detail can make much more sense of cash flow forecasts – in particular the level of

Managing your Bank and Bank Services

Table 5.4 NatWest BankLine Plus balance report as at 30 April 91. XYZ PLC Group

Account description	29 Apr 91 Closing ledger	29 Apr 91 Closing available	30 Apr 91 Current available	29 Apr 91 2 or more days' float
01497243(002) XYZ PLC Treasury a/c	600,000−	600,000−	600,000−	0
01497189(005) Parent company	148,634−	148,634−	114,305−	0
86571133(006) Subsidiary Co No 1	373,215	339,017	387,987	34,198
36486167(007) Subsidiary Co No 2	442,328	413,492	452,969	17,336
Net totals	66,909	3,875	126,651	51,534
Gross debits	748,634−	748,634−	714,305−	0
Gross credits	815,543	752,509	840,956	51,534

payments clearing in the current day can be precise and if arrangements have been made for say next-day clearing of cash, a precise figure can be obtained. Varying levels of detail can be agreed with the bank. However, balance reporting systems will not pick-up current-day transactions, which can include cheques presented across the counter.

Costs tend to be an initial fee followed by fixed monthly charges. The largest cost used to be the cost of the PC and printer – but many businesses can probably find a PC which can also be used for balance reporting.

Banks constantly change the range of products available and it is often worth describing a problem to your banker in case there is a product which could be adapted, but which is not immediately obvious.

Managing your Bank and Bank Services

Table 5.5 NatWest BankLine Plus previous day transaction report 29 Apr 91. XYZ PLC Group

01497189 – Parent company

Credits posted

4,500.00	IPS2187081201099 Sumitomo Bank
118.63	BS571310040
427.16	Cash cheques
135.21	Div 1389933 Brt Ord shares

5,181.00

Debits posted

1,534.45	Chq 30574
1,244.83	Chq 30586
474.35	Chq 30576
27,650.00	TF group salaries
8,258.00	TF group pensions

39,161.63

Conclusion

In summary, the relationship between a customer and its banker needs to be a partnership to be effective. While there are many opportunities to negotiate and control costs, these can only be taken so far. However, banks have a role to play in providing information about the business in a form that the business can use.

6
Liquidity and the Use of Deposit and Borrowing Instruments

- A brief description of various short-term deposit and borrowing instruments
- How to decide which instrument is appropriate for a given circumstance

This chapter will not review the detailed features of any particular instrument as these change all the time. Rather, the general characteristics of instruments are considered so that a decision can be taken on whether an instrument is likely to suit a particular requirement.

Given the concentration on liquidity, the instruments considered are generally short-term (i.e. with maturities of less than 1 year) but, as will be seen, borrowing *facilities* with maturities of greater than 1 year are frequently part of planning for future liquidity.

Deposit Instruments

The need to deposit will have been identified from a cash flow forecast. This will also have identified the amount available

Use of Deposit and Borrowing Instruments

and the period for which the funds are forecast to be available, and clearly these requirements will colour the selection of instrument. The main objectives of short-term investment will also be important:

- safety;
- liquidity;
- profitability.

(Note that the order in which these objectives is set out is critical. If a different priority is given to profitability, say, then there is the risk of total loss for a higher theoretical short-term gain.)

One of the most common types of problem in short-term depositing is the situation where funds are thought to be available for a given period, say 6 months, but there is a chance that they might be required sooner, say after 3 months. One way of dealing with this issue is to deposit for 3 months and then see what the position is like then. Alternatively, a 6 month instrument in which there is a liquid market could be selected if the return available seems particularly suitable. (A fuller consideration of this type of question is given in chapter 7.)

Bank deposits

Deposits with banks can be either made with the company's usual bank or through the wholesale markets with a different bank. In any event, the first requirement is to be satisfied with the credit standing of the bank (or, technically, other financial institutions such as building societies, licensed deposit-takers, savings and loans, etc.). As the collapse of BCCI has graphically shown, it is irresponsible to rely on any third party,

Use of Deposit and Borrowing Instruments

whether a broker or a central bank, unless that third party has given a formal guarantee. Further, for large sums, credit limits should be set in order to diversify risk.

The maturity of the deposit will be established at the time it is placed together with the rate of interest. Certainly, call deposits (that is, ones which may be withdrawn at no notice) will be available, but the return is likely to be that much lower. Therefore, call deposits are only suitable for smaller sums unsuitable for the wholesale markets.

Fixed-term deposits will be of the basic type considered in chapter 4, i.e. they will be for the given period with interest usually paid on maturity (although, for periods of greater than 6 months, interest may be paid 6-monthly). Also, other than in exceptional circumstances, they will not be repaid until the end of the period. Thus, if there is a chance that the funds will be required before the stated maturity of the deposit, then either a liquid instrument should have been chosen or a shorter period, or other sources of liquidity (e.g. borrowing facilities) should be available.

Certificates of Deposit

A certificate of deposit (CD) is a negotiable bearer instrument certificate issued by a bank or building society evidencing a deposit. These certificates may be traded in a fairly active secondary market and are priced as a function of the principal invested, the stated return on the CD and current money-market interest rates.

The interest rate payable upon maturity by the issuing institution is often lower than that available from a direct deposit because of the liquidity of the CD and may be up to $\frac{3}{8}$% p.a. below LIBID.

Use of Deposit and Borrowing Instruments

Although CDs offer useful liquidity, it is still preferable to anticipate holding them until maturity because of the risk of capital loss if they are sold prior to maturity. This capital loss arises usually because of the movement in interest rates. The liquidity of a particular CD depends upon the issuer – in the UK those of the clearing banks are most liquid, other banks are traded on a name-by-name basis which are often less liquid and therefore, higher yielding. Likewise, in the USA, CDs issued by the major US banks offer greatest liquidity.

Local authority and government bonds

These often have the liquidity characteristics of CDs, but the market for a particular issue may in itself not be particularly liquid. The returns available will vary by issue and, as always, the credit risk needs to be assessed. The most familiar government investments in the UK are *gilts*, but there are alternatives overseas, notably treasury bills in the USA.

Commercial paper

Commercial paper (CP) is a debt instrument issued by a company for a given period and with a fixed face value. The paper is issued at a discount to the face value representing the effective interest rate.

Typical returns are likely to be higher than for comparable bank deposits (other than for the most creditworthy multinational corporations) and this reflects the increased credit risk. Most investors will not have the skills or resources available to undertake the necessary regular credit evaluation, therefore CP programmes are frequently rated by credit-rating agencies such as Moodys, IBCA or Standard & Poors.

Use of Deposit and Borrowing Instruments

Investments might then only be made in CP issued by companies with a specified rating or better. This would not remove the credit risk.

Commercial paper can be liquid, but this depends upon the state of the market and, often, the quality of the issuer.

Bills of exchange

A bill of exchange is again an instrument evidencing a debt obligation, and bills of exchange were the traditional method of securing extended credit in international trade. The underlying credit risk on a bill rests with the obligor on the bill, but this may be enhanced by a financial institution *accepting* the bill (cf. bankers' acceptances).

Bills may be traded and they are priced on a discounted basis. In the UK, rates may often be attractive and an active market in certain types of bills known as eligible bills (because they have been accepted by a bank on the Bank of England's eligible list) is maintained by the discount houses. The rate of return available may sometimes be better than for an equivalent CD.

Ineligible bills tend to attract higher interest rates, but the risk is frequently greater and the market less liquid.

Different Currencies

Before considering borrowing instruments, the issue of investment in different currencies should be touched upon. Throughout, it has been assumed that investments have been made in one currency with a requirement for returns in that currency. It is clearly possible to introduce a further degree of

Use of Deposit and Borrowing Instruments

risk and seek higher returns by speculating on the future movement of exchange rates. Thus, a higher nominal return in a particular currency could be sought if the investor believed that that currency would not depreciate by more than the relative interest rate differential. But this needs to be a conscious decision and in considering liquidity management at this level it is best to remain in one currency and make decisions on that basis. If the necessary skills are available and the risk is deemed to be acceptable, then this is a further area of opportunity.

Obtaining and Selling Deposit Instruments

Having selected the type of instrument which most suits a given investment need, the same issues arise as are often the case when buying any product. Where can I buy it and how much will it cost?

For the small business, the clearing bank is the natural place to start – clearly they will offer their own products but an element of competition may be introduced by approaching a second bank. For small transactions it is often impractical and costly to shop around too much.

For larger transactions it is sensible to approach one of the banks' central dealing rooms. Here up-to-the-minute quotes may be obtained and consequently the most competitive price or interest rate. Transactions are all carried out over the telephone and are confirmed in writing afterwards. Competing quotes can thus be obtained from a number of banks for large transactions. In the USA, the largest issuers of CP issue their own CP directly and do not need to appoint dealers.

Use of Deposit and Borrowing Instruments

(This market is very substantial with total issues in excess of $100 billion p.a.) The use of banks and other traders will allow access to secondary markets, that is, instruments traded after their initial issue. The use of a secondary market should provide a firm assessment of current market prices.

A number of banks will trade in CDs and CP, if these are the favoured instruments. There are also a number of firms of money-brokers in the UK. Their role is to match borrowers and depositors and earn their return by deducting a commission (usually from the borrower). They do not take any credit risk themselves, nor do they offer advice (as local authorities in the UK will now have realized following the collapse of BCCI).

It is often sensible to start with the company's own clearing or merchant bank before going out too widely if the particular arrangements for an instrument are unfamiliar. However, investors should always be clear about the liquidity of a particular instrument when buying it – that is, can it be sold before maturity (and, if so, how?) or does it have to be (or is it preferable to be) held until maturity?

Borrowing Instruments

The essential feature of borrowing as it affects liquidity is the *availability* of borrowed funds when they are required. The consideration of borrowing instruments in this book looks at the marginal borrowing facilities. It does not look at structural long-term debt such as institutional debt or long-term committed facilities as these are fundamental to the basic capital structure decision facing any company.

Use of Deposit and Borrowing Instruments

Overdrafts

One of the great advantages of the UK banking system is the availability of overdrafts. These are lines of credit made available on ordinary current accounts to companies at slightly more expensive rates than can be obtained through other markets, but which are repayable on demand. In practice, the demand feature is rarely used and some form of notice of withdrawal may be anticipated. Their great benefit is the flexibility which is afforded in the management of very short-term liquidity.

Thus if the cash forecast shows a surplus for the current day of, say, £500,000 but that there is a risk that the figure may vary by £250,000 then the availability of an overdraft facility will allow the company to deposit £750,000 but run the risk of an overdrawn balance of up to £500,000. Given all possible outcomes, we can see that this is the preferred course of action. If we assume that overnight deposit rates are 10% and that the overdraft costs 12% and we look at the three cases of actual balances of £250,000, £500,000 and £750,000, then the net interest receipts are as shown in table 6.1. If we compare this with the alternative safe position of just depositing £250,000 (assuming that we cannot go overdrawn), we see that we receive just £68.49 and with the possibility of £250,000 or £500,000 on a non-interest-bearing account.

Therefore, the potential loss of £27.39 if the balance turns out at the pessimistic end does not match the gain of £136.99 at the optimistic end. For major companies, where these decisions are taken over millions, the gains can be very significant. Furthermore, the process of cash forecasting should give an increasingly good feel for the margin of error, which may not be the same each day, and this will increase the benefit of the overdraft.

Use of Deposit and Borrowing Instruments

Table 6.1 Use of overdrafts

	Actual balance		
	£250,000	£500,000	£750,000
Interest on deposit of £750,000	£205.48	£205.48	£205.48
Overdraft cost on balance	£164.38	£82.19	0
Net interest	£41.10	£123.29	£205.48

In spite of the flexibility of the overdraft, for companies which are experiencing liquidity problems, the overdraft cannot be the sole source of finance because of its on-demand nature. There need to be other sources, but for companies where the actual level of cash is difficult to forecast, it is a particularly useful tool.

Committed and uncommitted facilities

Although loan facilities may be expressed to be available for a given period, drawings are frequently for shorter interest maturities and the selection of any particular interest period mirrors the decisions taken for deposits.

Of great significance for liquidity management is the difference between uncommitted and committed facilities. In the case of committed facilities, provided that the terms and conditions of the loan agreement have been complied with, the lender is obliged to advance the funds – this is not the case for uncommitted facilities.

The balance of committed and uncommitted facilities depends very much on the financial standing of the borrower. If the company is a small engineering company, then it will be preferable to ensure the availability of finance by negotiating a high level of committed facilities for the final £2 million or so – there is clearly not this requirement for large, financially stable corporations (although this may be so in a given overseas subsidiary where there is little liquidity in the domestic market).

Commercial paper

The main features of CP were described above and there are further restrictions in particular countries (especially in the sterling CP market, where the Bank of England has set limits on the size of company which can issue CP). In terms of the management of liquidity, CP may be regarded as a diversified source of uncommitted finance. It is useful to seek sources of funds outside the banking markets in order to leave credit room with the banks for other facilities (particularly as banks increasingly control their use of capital), but there is also the risk that the liquidity of the CP market will evaporate at precisely the point that funds are most needed. Therefore, the treasurer will need to be aware of other sources of finance for these eventualities.

The other great benefit of CP is that it tends to cost less than comparable bank loans. Commercial paper, in the form of negotiable bearer instruments, is issued through banks who act as dealers for the issuer who then place it with mainly non-bank investors. The dealers retain no exposure to the issuer once they have sold the paper. Typical maturities are 1,

2, 3 or 6 months. However, in the UK, CP may be issued for any period between 7 and 364 days and there are often shorter periods in order to suit an issuer's requirements.

The limits set on companies by the Bank of England for the sterling CP market are:

- Companies must have net assets of over £25 million, and
- Have shares or debt listed in London, or
- Have shares or debt listed on an authorized exchange, or
- Be incorporated in the UK.

Companies who are not themselves eligible can issue paper if it is guaranteed by a company which would be eligible in its own right, or by a bank. Commercial paper can also be issued by building societies and certain local authorities in England and Wales.

There are relatively modest costs associated with issuing CP by way of fees to the issuing and paying agent for handling the notes themselves. Additionally there will be printing costs for circulating mini-prospectuses to investors and also for the notes. The dealers themselves will usually earn their commission by making a profit between the buying and selling price ('making a turn') when the paper is issued.

A more substantial cost, both in time and money, will arise if it is decided to seek a credit rating (see above). Credit ratings are more common now and are obligatory in the domestic US CP market.

Sterling bankers' acceptances

The consideration of cost is very important in looking at raising debt and as liquidity diminishes, the cost consequently rises both due to scarcity of supply and also due to the increased risk of failure of the borrower.

Use of Deposit and Borrowing Instruments

For companies with sufficient trade related activity (as defined by the Bank of England), drawing bills of exchange on themselves and then having them *accepted* by an eligible bank can often be a cheaper way of raising debt than by borrowing directly from a bank.

Marginal sources of liquidity

When a company cannot borrow directly (or if it becomes prohibitively expensive), then the need to keep the company trading becomes paramount. At the extreme, this is real liquidity management in practice.

The control of working capital often becomes the issue. This may mean stretching payments to suppliers. Many companies will do this, but there is often a trade-off between prompt payment and receipt of discounts. At the other extreme, a steady increase in trade terms may lead to suppliers withdrawing their goods or, worse, to a general belief that the company is about to fail.

There will also be a reduction in costs and stocks. In the final extreme, cash will need to be raised by selling assets. For many companies the assets owned may be illiquid (such as land and buildings), but there may also be the option of *factoring* receivables. This will involve selling the right to receive the cash due from receivables in return for a discounted amount up front. This can be an expensive method of raising cash, but may be the only solution available. In certain countries where the banking system is still based heavily on trade, this may indeed be the normal way of raising finance.

Obtaining Borrowing Instruments

The critical difference in obtaining borrowing instruments, as compared to deposit instruments, is that the lender/investor will need to be willing to take a credit risk on the borrower/issuer. Consequently, banks will have a target market in mind and the chances are that the bank will try to market these instruments to the company, but at least the company should begin to understand what the bank is describing.

In any event, the prospective lender should always be able to present its business and its financial requirements in a clear manner. This is often the reason that otherwise sound businesses do not obtain the facilities that they need and could command.

7
Managing Interest Rate Risk

> - An explanation of the various instruments available to hedge movements in interest rates
> - How to identify which instrument is suitable in a given situation

In chapter 4, the concept of interest rate risk was introduced. This is the exposure that the results of a business have to movements in interest rates. At its simplest, we can all understand that if borrowings are on a floating rate basis, then an increase in interest rates will reduce the profits of the business. There is also the concept of the opportunity cost of fixed interest rates: if a business places a deposit for a long period at fixed interest rates, then an increase in interest rates will represent a lost opportunity, especially if competitors are able to exploit this increase in a way that the business in question cannot. Finally, if an increase in interest rates means that customers are less inclined to buy the business' products or services, then there is an *economic exposure* to interest rates. For the purposes of this chapter, we will concentrate on the first example above of interest rate risk.

There are a number of books and a lot of bank marketing literature which deal with the details of the various instruments available to manage interest rate risk; this chapter will not, therefore, go into too much detail. It will, however,

Managing Interest Rate Risk

consider the various situations in which a particular instrument might be suitable.

For businesses operating within tight financial constraints and uncertain cash projections, the exposure to interest rate risk can prove the final straw. Therefore, the practical use of instruments which secure a future interest rate without the associated obligation to borrow or deposit is particularly helpful. But for many businesses, the most basic way to manage interest rate risk is to borrow on either a fixed or floating rate basis. Therefore, it is normal to establish a proportion of borrowings (or deposits if there are especially large surpluses) which is desired to be at fixed rates. For small companies, this proportion is likely to be fairly high given the need for predictability – but the ability to secure fixed-rate debt is often limited by the unwillingness of lenders to advance funds for long periods or on a committed basis.

For very large companies, the proportion of fixed-rate debt will form part of the basic decision on capital structure and will also be tied in to the level of gearing. However, the proportion of fixed-rate debt is frequently associated with the income profile of a business. Thus, a leasing company with income streams linked to fixed interest rates will wish to reduce its exposure by having a high level of fixed-rate debt.

In the end, the decision has to be a practical one based on the nature of the business, the perceived level of risk that the company wishes to accept and what can actually be transacted in the financial markets.

Forward Forwards

In chapter 4, the techniques of disaggregating interest rates were explained – this resulted in establishing the market's view of interest rates for a given future period. This can be taken one step further to calculate a forward forward interest rate, that is, the rate at which a bank agrees to lend for a given period at some stage in the future.

Before the development of the instruments described later in this chapter, the rate for a loan for 3 months in 3 months' time was established by lending for 6 months, but redepositing for the first 3 months. The calculations would be as explained for disaggregation, but the forward forward rate would be calculated by using the 6-month offer and 3-month bid. This clearly results in some fairly wide spreads and by the time that the bank adds on the costs for using its balance sheet, the rates tend to become unattractive.

Forward Rate Agreements (FRAs)

An FRA is an agreement whereby two parties agree to *fix* the interest rate on a loan or deposit for a given future period on a set amount. On maturity, if actual interest rates are different from the rate set under the FRA, then the effective interest differential (discounted for early receipt) passes between the two parties.

A buyer of an FRA is the party wishing to protect itself against a future rise in interest rates, while the seller of the FRA wishes to protect itself against a future fall in interest rates. Therefore, a buyer of an FRA is a borrower and a seller of an FRA is a lender or investor.

No commitment is made by either party to lend or borrow the principal amount. The principal sum is not at risk as the exposure to both parties is the interest differential between the agreed rate and the settlement rate at maturity. The use of

Managing Interest Rate Risk

an FRA is probably best demonstrated by the following example.

It is currently 1 January and Company X has a borrowing requirement of $10 million for 6 months from 1 June. Interest rates are currently 8.43% for 6 months. Company X wishes to protect itself against a rise in interest rates and can achieve this by buying a 5 v 11 FRA. (Note that 5 v 11 means an FRA for a period which begins in 5 months' time and ends in 11 months' time.) On 1 January no money moves but Company X buys the FRA with an agreed rate of 8.62%. This represents the effective interest rate at which X will borrow for 6 months from 1 June.

At 1 June, interest rates have increased by 1% to 9.43% and therefore X is due to receive a settlement from the bank. The settlement is calculated as follows:

$$\frac{(0.0943 - 0.0862) \times 10{,}000{,}000 \times 182/360}{1 + (0.0943 \times 182/360)} = \$39{,}085.62$$

This represents the interest differential between current 6-month rates (9.43%) and the agreed rate under the FRA (8.43%) on the principal sum ($10 million) for the period of the protection (6 months or, precisely, 182 days on the basis of a 360-day year), but discounted from 1 December to 1 June representing the convention that interest is normally paid at the end of the period.

We can confirm that the effective interest rate to X is in reality 8.62%.

On 1 June X receives	+ 39,086
On 1 June X borrows	+9,960,914
(i.e. 10,000,000 less the FRA receipt)	
On 1 December borrowing is repaid	−9,960,914
On 1 December interest at 9.43% paid	− 474,876

Or, to put these together, in $:

1 June   +10,000,000
1 December   −10,435,790

Effective interest rate from 1 June to 1 December is therefore

$$\frac{10,000,000}{435,790} \times 100 \times \frac{360}{182} = 8.62\% \text{ p.a.}$$

(Note that a 360-day year was used throughout as we were dealing with US dollars.)

The effect of using an FRA is to fix the interest rate, and therefore, the treasurer needs to be relatively certain that the underlying cash flows will arise. In this sense, the use of FRAs provides a certain way of arranging fixed interest rates in the short to medium term.

Financial Futures

A financial futures contract is an agreement to buy or sell a standard quantity of a specific financial instrument (say, 3 month Eurodollar interest rates) at a predetermined future date, and at a price agreed between the parties through open outcry on the floor of an organized exchange (e.g. the International Money Market in Chicago or LIFFE in London).

The purchase or sale of a financial futures contract is a commitment to make or take delivery of a specific financial instrument at a predetermined date in the future, for which the price is established at the time of initial execution. For example, the purchase of a June 3-month Eurodollar contract commits the purchaser (if the contract is not sold in the market in the meantime) to make a deposit or to take a rate on a notional deposit of 1 million Eurodollars in June for 3 months at an agreed interest rate implicit in the price. (Note: the actual procedure depends upon the exchange being used, but in practice settlement is often avoided by buying or selling a matching contract.)

A member buying or selling a futures contract is required to lodge a deposit with the clearing house of the exchange called the initial or deposit margin. This is a fixed amount per contract and must be left in place as long as the position is held. In addition, daily variation margin is received from, or paid to, the clearing house as the position generates unrealized profits or losses as market prices move. In practice the actual obligation to deposit or lend is often satisfied by the sale or purchase of the appropriate contract at maturity.

Financial futures have the severe limitations for many companies of complex administration and monitoring requirements. Furthermore, the standardized nature of the contracts means that they rarely match a particular requirement to borrow or deposit whether in amount or period.

In practice, they achieve the same end result as FRAs, i.e. they fix a future interest rate, and indeed FRAs are in effect repackaged futures prepared by banks to suit their customers' precise requirements (in addition to the two-way trading in FRAs themselves).

Swaps and Longer-term Instruments

Interest rate (and currency) swaps have become a very familiar feature of the international capital markets since the mid–1980s. The basic feature of an interest rate swap is an agreement between two parties to exchange interest rates on two different bases on an agreed principal sum over a defined future period.

The most common example is the fixed floating swap. This is a method whereby one party will agree to make a series of floating-rate interest payments based on a short-term interest rate (say 6-month LIBOR), and the other party will make a series of fixed-rate payments based on a long-term interest rate. In practice, on each payment date the payments are netted against each other so that only the party owing the greater amount makes the net payment. In a swap involving only one currency, no principal is exchanged.

The great benefit of swaps for many small and medium-sized companies has been the ability to raise what is, in effect, fixed-rate debt at times when the traditional fixed-rate debt markets could not be accessed by companies of their size. More widely, all companies can change the interest profile of their liabilities without needing to raise fresh debt.

Caps, Floors and Collars

While swaps fix interest rates for future dates, it is also possible to limit interest cost or interest income by using caps and floors respectively. These are packaged interest rate option products.

In the case of a cap, in return for a premium, a bank will agree to pay a company the interest differential based on a set principal if a given interest rate (say 6-month LIBOR) is above an agreed fixed rate (e.g. 14%) on certain fixed dates. Conversely, a floor operates *below* a set rate and therefore is used to protect interest income.

Managing Interest Rate Risk

In order to minimize the premia required for floors and caps a company might agree to limit any benefit received from falling interest rates (if using a cap) by paying to the bank the interest differential if rates fall below a set level (e.g. 12%). Thus, the company could be assured that its interest cost would fall between the two levels (e.g. 12 and 14%). This is known as a *collar*. Caps, floors and collars can be shown diagrammatically as in figure 7.1.

Caps, floors and collars are not restricted to just the medium and long term, they can be used for shorter periods, although this is not their normal use. A collar over 6 months may be regarded as a low-cost option (see below), while certain UK clearing banks are attempting to introduce base rate caps and base rate FRAs (i.e. those which limit the cost of base rates) for their smaller corporate customers.

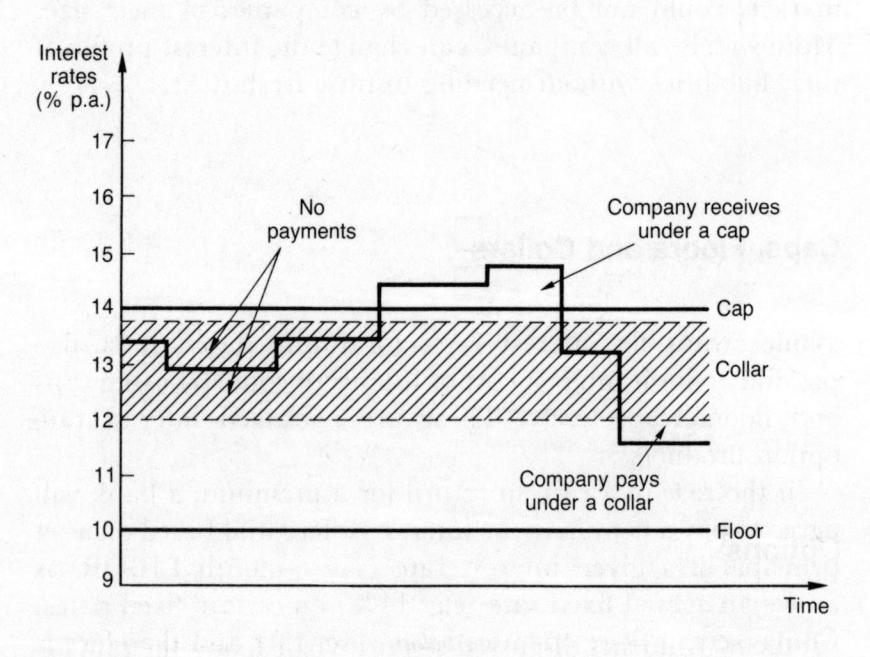

Figure 7.1 Caps, floors and collars

Managing Interest Rate Risk

Clearly, the cost of the cap, floor or collar increases the overall cost of borrowing for the period when no payment is received and in the case of a collar this can be seen diagrammatically as in figure 7.2.

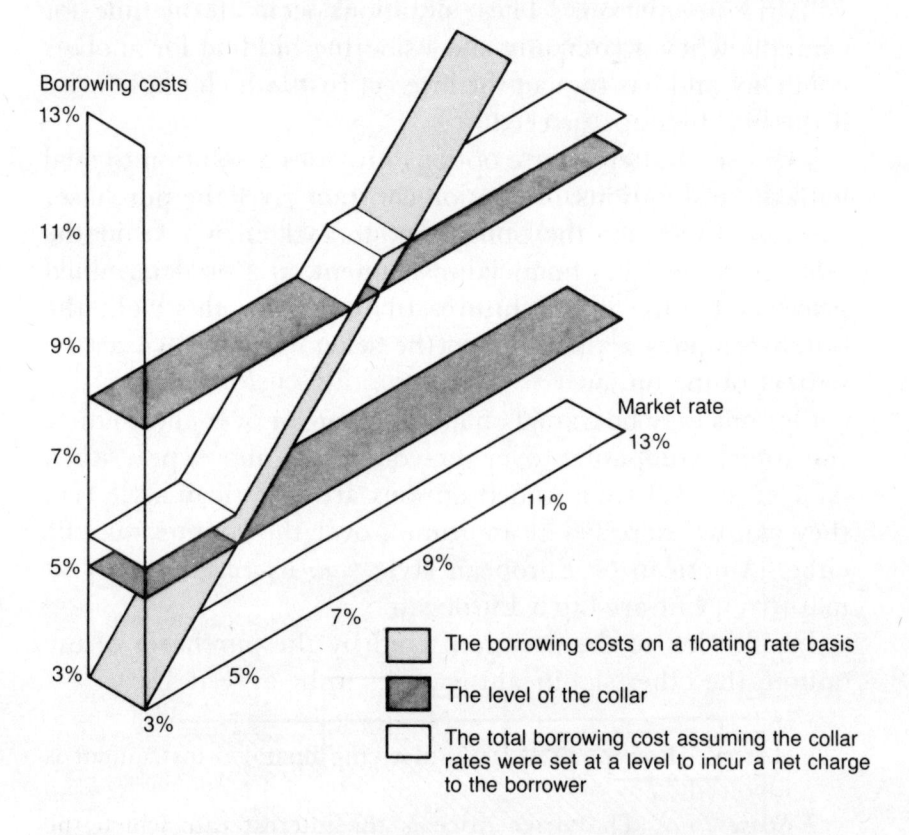

Figure 7.2 Interest rate collar

Options

All the instruments discussed so far involve fixing the rate for future obligations. These work well in an environment where

Managing Interest Rate Risk

future cash flows are predictable or where there are clear obligations. However, what can a company do when an increase in interest rates would place undue pressure on a business and where it is unclear whether certain cash flows will arise in any event? These situations occur all the time, for example when a company is considering bidding for another company and has to plan the interest costs which might arise if the bid does not succeed.

The use of interest rate options provides a solution to deal with these situations. An option contract gives the purchaser the right, but not the obligation, to lock in a rate in the relevant underlying financial instrument, at a predetermined price, at a time in the future. In return for this right the purchaser pays a premium to the seller (also known as the writer) of the option.

Options may be traded on an exchange or over-the-counter (for most companies over-the-counter is more practical). Almost all exchange traded options are American style (i.e. they can be exercised at any time); over-the-counter may be either American or European style (i.e. exercisable only at maturity), but are often European.

In addition to the premium paid by the purchaser of the option, the other significant features to be agreed are:

1 *Amount*. How much of the underlying financial instrument is involved.
2 *Strike Price*. The strike price is the interest rate which the holder of the option has the right to receive:
   (a) at the money – strike price equal to current market forward rates;
   (b) in the money – strike price more advantageous to buyer than current market rates (higher premium);
   (c) out of the money – strike price less favourable to buyer than current market rates (lower premium).

Managing Interest Rate Risk

3 *Type of option.* There are broadly two styles of options. American-style options can be exercised at any time up to the expiry date or European-style options which can only be exercised on fixed dates.

The pricing of options is a complicated subject which commands a book in itself. Once the strike price has been established, the other great determinant is how volatile the market is perceived to be over the period of the option. For the user of the option the best approach is to regard the option as insurance and to compare the cost with other alternatives available.

Example

If we return to the example used to explain FRAs on p.86, another solution might have been to hedge the borrowing requirement by an option. In this case the company would have bought a call option on 6-month Eurodollar LIBOR. If the strike price were, say 8.5% with a premium of 0.175% p.a., then the calculation would have been.

Premium: 10,000,000 × 0.00175 × 151/360 = $7340.27

By 1 June, interest rates are higher than the strike price. Therefore, it is profitable to exercise the option and to borrow at 8.5%. If we ignore the funding costs of the option premium, total costs are

10,000,000 × 0.085 × 182/360 = $429,722.22 + $7340.27
= $437,062.49

to give an effective interest rate of 8.645% p.a. compared with the cost of 8.62% p.a. using FRAs.

Managing Interest Rate Risk

All other things being equal, options should be expected to be more expensive than FRAs or futures because of the additional flexibility. Many companies find the up-front premia unacceptable particularly in an environment of cost-cutting. However, if this is compared to general insurance and placed in the context of overall interest costs, a reasonable strategy can be developed.

In an environment when future cash flows are uncertain and a company wishes both to limit its interest rate exposure and to fix the cash outlay if funds do not arise, then options provide a relatively straightforward peace-of-mind solution.

Use of Hedging Instruments

The decision about which instrument to use revolves around two questions:

1. Does the company want to *fix* the interest rate or to know its worst rate?
2. How certain are the future cash flows?

Worst-rate instruments are options, floors, caps and collars. FRAs, futures and swaps fix interest rates.

If cash flows are certain, then the decision to fix an interest rate can be taken with more comfort as this provides an environment in which the business can plan. There is often the opportunity to borrow at a fixed rate in the first place and, therefore, not worry about these techniques. But for future periods or for small amounts or non-standard periods, these instruments can provide that certainty.

Where cash flows are uncertain, there may still be a need to fix future rates, particularly if the uncertainty arises from potentially poor trading (cf. chapter 8), as this gives a lower-cost solution than for options.

Two simple examples are considered below.

Company D

This has a borrowing programme of $100 million which is currently all based on floating rates. The loans are from a variety of banks and the programme is expected to last 5 years. Roll-overs are due in 3 months' time.

The central questions here are: how much fixed-rate debt does the company want and what is its current view of interest rates?

1 If it believes that rates might rise, it could decide to take out an interest rate swap on part of its debt (say 50%).
2 If it believes that rates might rise in the short term, but then fall again, it could take out FRAs or options in the short term or buy a swap for less than 5 years.
3 If it believes that rates will fall, it could leave all its debt on a floating basis but protect itself by buying a cap at a highish rate for a relatively low premium.

These are not the only strategies, but I hope that they begin to show the number of choices available. Note also that the view on interest rates is central to the strategy to be adopted. Of course, an overriding policy decision might be taken to have a certain proportion of debt at fixed rates – in which case there may be an issue of tactical timing on when to fix. In any event, once a strategy has been adopted, that is not the end of it. Conditions change and therefore there needs to be a constant review to ensure that overall objectives continue to be met.

Company E

This is a small business trading near the limits of its borrowing facilities, and it has monthly cash flow difficulties. It is exposed to a potential trading downturn in a few months' time which would be made worse by an increase in interest rates.

In this case, the clear requirement is to limit the interest cost. A small company may be unable to obtain options, but more importantly unable to pay the premia in the short term. Therefore, the use of FRAs if the bank will agree to these would be desirable or, failing that, just fixed-rate debt.

The real problem in this type of situation is that, no matter what the theoretical solution, the practical problems of obtaining the necessary instrument or credit approval will limit room for manœuvre.

A Note on Taxation

As with all treasury matters, the taxation consequences need to be considered carefully. Not only do local taxation regimes dictate the particular company to be used to ensure deduction for payments made, but the after-tax interest cost must be considered.

In particular, although payments under swaps, FRAs and options may attract a deduction for taxation, the effective cost needs to recognize that there may be a timing mismatch between allowance for these payments and for interest (which can be on a paid basis). However, these consequences can cloud the basic issue of whether or not to hedge for many smaller companies.

8
Liquidity Management in Practice

- Putting the theory into practice
- Some simple case studies

The principal objective of liquidity management is always to *maintain liquidity* so that a company or organization (or for that matter an individual) can continue to meet its commercial objectives. But there is also the task of managing the liquidity in an optimal way in the best interests of the organization.

The general approach to liquidity management in practice has already been set out as safety, liquidity and profitability, to which can now be added the management of risk. By putting all these together we can now address the practical question of: how much, for how long, what instrument and for what return? But liquidity management cannot be reduced to one decision, say, to invest in a CD for 3 months at 10% and to leave it at that. The dynamics of both the market-place and the underlying business mean that decisions need to be kept under active review to ensure that overall objectives (and especially the principal objective of maintaining liquidity) continue to be met.

Liquidity Management in Practice

The General Approach

In earlier chapters the various concepts and tools used in liquidity management have been described – we can now put these together to see how decisions might operate in relatively complicated situations.

The starting-point is to develop a cash forecast for a given future period and then look at it critically in the context of the business. This will give certain alternatives for funding or depositing, both in terms of amount and period. Interest periods can then be selected against a view of interest rates, leading to a selection of market and instrument. If need be, future interest rates can be hedged to deal with uncertainty (either against movement in rates or in cash flow). The resulting decision is then kept under review and the process repeated each time there is a change in circumstances. The flow chart in figure 8.1 sets out the process in a simplified way.

In order to demonstrate the process in practice, let us consider some cases and look at the alternative decisions that can be taken at each stage.

Seasonal PLC

Seasonal PLC is a retailer where sales are made for cash and arise in two main selling seasons. Goods are purchased up to 3 months ahead of sale, but orders are placed many months before this and there is limited opportunity to cancel orders once placed. Costs are predictable and not linked to the level of sales.

Liquidity Management in Practice

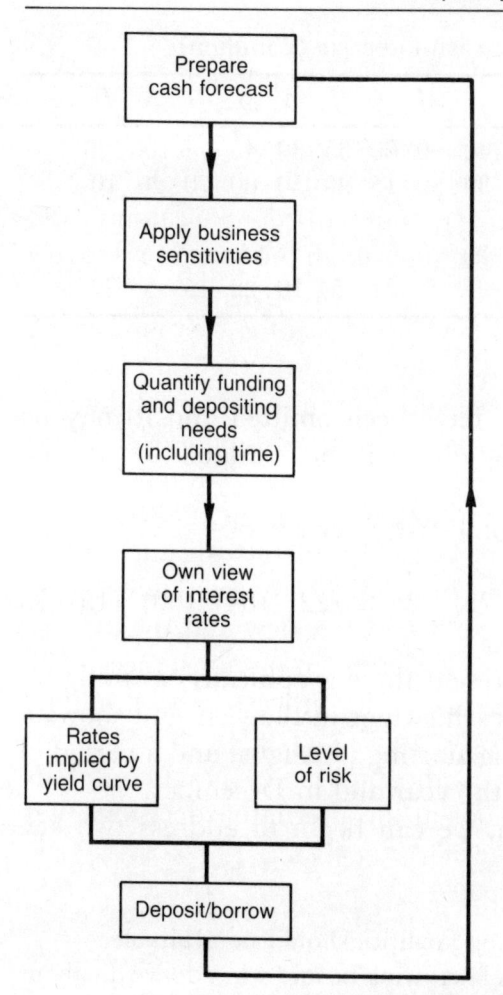

Figure 8.1 The process of liquidity management

The cash forecast (prepared on a receipts and payments basis) at the beginning of the year was as shown in table 8.1. The opening balance at the beginning of January was £40m borrowed. (Note: in order to simplify the example, capital

Liquidity Management in Practice

Table 8.1 Seasonal PLC: cash forecasts (£ million)

	J	F	M	A	M	J	J	A	S	O	N	D
Sales	80	30	32	40	40	60	35	30	45	74	100	120
Purchases	5	15	40	30	30	15	20	50	80	70	20	10
Tax			25									
Dividends				20				5				
Costs	5	5	22	5	5	22	5	10	22	10	5	22

expenditure and interest have been omitted and it may be assumed that separate funding will be available to manage the exposures.)

These forecasts give total cash forecasts of:

(40) 30 40 (15) (30) (25) (2) 8 (22) (84) (90) (15) 73

It is often helpful to represent these graphically, as in figure 8.2. This highlights the cash swings in the year and shows a period of heavy borrowing starting in August and a period of modest surplus early in the year and in December.

With this information, we can begin to address two key questions:

1 What level of borrowing facilities should be available?
2 How long should each borrowing be and what do we do about interest rate risk?

First, we need to consider the cash forecast carefully. Assume that sufficient care has been taken in its preparation (although in practice this should not always be assumed). The following points need to be noted. It is not clear whether sales and purchases move evenly with each other in a month.

Liquidity Management in Practice

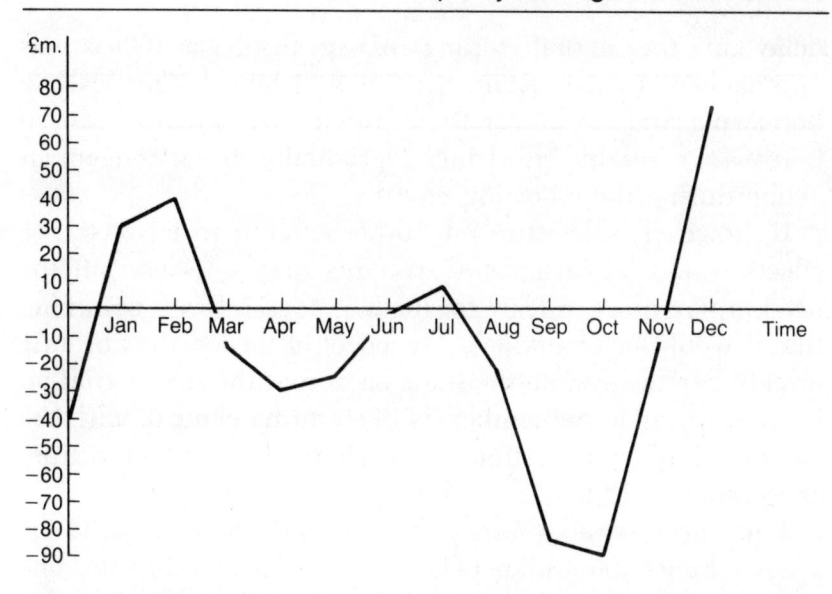

Figure 8.2 Seasonal PLC: total cash forecasts

Given the evidence that purchases are bought well in advance of sales, it may be possible that during September and October, in particular, the peak borrowing requirement may exceed the month-end position and thus approach £150 million.

Next, it is necessary to look at the sensitivity of the cash forecast. If sales turn out to be lower than forecast, then the usual response will be to reduce the intake of stock to match the lower sales level. If the sales downturn becomes apparent only during September, there may be little that can be done about orders for stock already placed. Thus the effect of a 15% reduction in sales forecast (not so unusual in the recession in the UK of 1989–91) would be to increase the absolute year-end borrowings by £50 million. The exact phasing of this would also depend on whether there was any

Liquidity Management in Practice

delay in the actual timing of spending as Christmas approached. In any event, there would be a higher level of borrowing and for longer than anticipated. The increase in borrowings might be reduced gradually by management action during the following months.

If, however, sales turn out to be better than forecast, the effects would be earlier cash receipts than forecast, but the need to pay more quickly for further stock (always assuming that it would be available). The effect of this on the absolute level of borrowings, on the same basis that the sales variation becomes clear in September, is likely to be neutral, with the likelihood of a reduction by perhaps £25 million during September and October and from December onwards.

The effect of all these points is that there need to be approaching £200 million of facilities available to be safe. The majority of these will not be needed until September and should be repaid by the end of the year. Since this pattern clearly recurs each year, it would be sensible to have at least £50 million available by way of a committed facility for, say, 5 years and which can also be drawn and repaid at will. In order to arrange the remaining facilities, bankers will need a very clear view that these are the ongoing seasonal requirements of the business so that they will not be surprised at the level of borrowings later in the year.

The second question dealt with periods of borrowing and interest rate risk. Current interest rates are shown in table 8.2. It can be seen from the general shape of the yield curve and by disaggregating that the market expects interest rates to fall gently over the coming year. However, there is considerable room for change and the trend is by no means clear – in particular, the rates for certain interest periods may be driven by the liquidity in the market for that period (especially for unusual periods such as 9 months).

Liquidity Management in Practice

Table 8.2 Seasonal PLC: current interest rates

Months	%
1	$10\frac{1}{2} - \frac{1}{4}$
2	$10\frac{1}{2} - \frac{1}{4}$
3	$10\frac{3}{4} - \frac{1}{2}$
6	$10\frac{3}{4} - \frac{1}{2}$
9	$10\frac{7}{8} - \frac{5}{8}$
12	$10\frac{3}{4} - \frac{1}{2}$

If we look back at figure 8.2, there are a number of funding alternatives. These include:

1. borrowing or depositing for the longest period suitable – so, for example, borrowing £25 million for 3 months at the end of August and incrementally thereafter.
2. Borrowing £25 million in April for around 8 months and depositing any short-term surpluses in the meantime.

In fact, there are a large number of complex options which arise. However, it is often better to keep it simple by maintaining a broad overview. The essential feature about this business is the very steep exposure to the cost of borrowing in the second half.

First, it is helpful to calculate the market's expectation of borrowing rates at the end of the year by disaggregating the 3-month rate in 9 months' time. This is calculated as

$$(1 + im) = 1.1075/(1 + 0.10875 \times 9/12)$$
$$= 1.02398$$

i.e. the 3-month rate in 9 months' time is expected to be of the order of 9.6% (2.398 × 4).

Liquidity Management in Practice

Compared to current rates, this fall would be beneficial, but Seasonal PLC would need to set its own view of rates against this. Every 1% movement in rates over the period August – November would mean around £132,500 in interest cost. While this is a large amount, it is not going to be critical to the future existence of the company. However, there is a clear opportunity to manage the future interest cost.

Therefore, if FRAs (either 8 v 11 or 9 v 12, i.e. for periods of 3 months to begin in either 8 or 9 months time and to end in 11 or 12 months' time) can be bought at under 10%, it might be prudent to do so unless there is a very strong view that rates might fall further. If there is that belief, then protection could be obtained by purchasing 3-month interest rate options to expire in 8 or 9 months' time.

The essential feature from this point is to keep the situation under review. Cash forecasts will continue to be prepared and these should show any significant variance to expectations. In particular, a deterioration in sales will allow the following action:

- early revision of purchases;
- further protection against rising rates;
- if need be, the negotiation of further facilities.

In effect, it is likely that the first sign of trouble will be identified in the treasury department and it will require some diplomacy to persuade other colleagues of the need for action.

In chapter 3 we met Seasonal PLC before, when considering how to look at variations in forecast. The original forecast for the months of October to December was

$$(90) \quad (15) \quad 73$$

but turned out to be:

$$(110) \quad (50) \quad 20$$

Liquidity Management in Practice

In practice, as October approached, better information would have shown the need to borrow more and for longer, but with the same result of cash positive by the end of the year. On the basis that the facilities had been arranged, Seasonal PLC would have the alternatives of borrowing for 1, 2 or 3 months depending on its view of the interest rates available at the time. Again, in practice, unless the view on rates was held very strongly, two reasonable approaches would have been either to borrow for the longest period for which funds were expected to be available or to average over time by choosing a mixture of the periods available.

So, overall, Seasonal PLC could manage all the information available to it – the cash flows as they changed, the interest rates currently available and its own expectations and also the hedging instruments and borrowing facilities available to ensure both that the necessary liquidity was available and that it was managed in the most efficient manner.

International Cruises Inc.

This company operates in two divisions. The largest division is the shipping division which is capital-intensive and is highly geared by loans which are secured on the ships owned by the division (rather like mortgaging houses). The shipping division receives its income from shipping cargo, but also from trading in the value of its ships, which have been rising due to undersupply.

The other division is the tourism division which generates strong cash flow by selling holidays and taking deposits in the early part of the year, but only paying suppliers (airlines, hoteliers) later in the year. This division is profitable.

In addition to the loans secured on the ships, the group is funded by overdrafts and unsecured loans totalling $50

Liquidity Management in Practice

million. These facilities are on demand are reviewed each October after the main season. It is now December and the facilities are in place (albeit on an on-demand basis) for the coming months. As is usual, the cash flow from the tourism division is planned to support the activities of the shipping division.

Cash forecasts for the coming months are as shown in table 8.3. It is clear that the company can only just live within its facilities and is dependent on the early cash receipt from a ship sale and the continuing cash flow from the tourism division. It is also clear that, during this part of the year, the main shipping activity is a cash drain (indeed it is only likely to break even in the early part of the year). The continuing drain in cash terms of the shipping division is being financed by the tourism division and also by ship trading (although $10 million will be required to meet the first instalment of a new ship during April).

In this environment, many of the more normal issues in liquidity management, such as choice of interest period, become secondary to ensuring continuing cash flow. The ship loans will be at fixed interest rates, therefore those cash flows

Table 8.3 International Cruises Inc: cash forecasts ($ million)

	Dec.	Jan.	Feb.	Mar.	April	May
Opening position	(30)					
Tourism	5	5	10	10	15	20
Shipping	(8)	(8)	(18)	(18)	(16)	(3)
Ship trading and interest	(2)	23	(2)	(2)	(12)	(2)
Closing position	(35)	(15)	(25)	(35)	(48)	(33)
Agreed facilities	(50)	(50)	(50)	(50)	(50)	(50)

are predictable, but the company is heavily exposed to both an increase in interest rates and to a downturn in business. In situations where the central issue is going to be a lack of liquidity and where there is an exposure to rising interest rates, the best course of action would be to draw loans for the *longest period possible*. (Note: the treasurer and relevant directors should always be aware of the ethical and legal considerations of drawing loans for long periods – or, indeed, any period – if they have misled bankers as to the true position or if there is a risk of trading while insolvent. There is a fine line between ethical actions and the risk of making a business needlessly bankrupt.) This action removes the risk that an already difficult situation might be worsened by an additional pressure.

But in this case, the chief financial officer (CFO), treasurer or other manager responsible for the liquidity of the group will need to anticipate what else could be done. In practice, the banks would not withdraw their facilities as that act alone would force the business to cease trading – their repayment would come from normal receipts. However, it is equally unlikely that further facilities are going to be available without good reason. In this context, the underlying profitability and future viability of the group become critical.

There are two significant sensitivities here:

1 the receipt of $25 million;
2 the certainty of receipts from tourism.

If the $25 million is delayed for, say, 3 months (and this is entirely possible – delay in negotiations, lack of finance for the purchaser, collapse in ship values, etc.), then the group will be at the limit of its facilities in February and will exceed them from March onwards. Any room which might be available in February would be removed if there were the

Liquidity Management in Practice

slightest slippage in tourism receipts. Action therefore needs to be taken now to arrange further finance. Management of working capital should already be tight – involving stretching payables and attempting to accelerate receivables.

Otherwise, there are four ways to improve the cash position:

1 raise equity;
2 negotiate further debt;
3 sell assets;
4 cancel capital expenditure.

In a situation where the position is marginal, all four should be attempted simultaneously. The sale of assets may take a long time (and a major asset is the tourism division), but there could be a good case for sales at bargain prices, although this can give too clear a message to the outside world. If there is no cash available, then capital expenditure cannot be paid for, but contingency plans need to be prepared to handle the $10 million payment due in April. This will involve anticipating the supplier's reaction to delaying delivery.

However, the major efforts will need to be directed at raising either equity or debt. Both have the problem of the viability of the business, in particular the cash outflow of the shipping division. Investors and lenders will need a clear statement of the management action to be taken to improve the position. This plan needs to be available or else funds are highly unlikely to be made available – indeed a reporting accountants' report may be required. All this will take time which means that efforts need to be placed in three areas:

1 ensuring the earliest receipt of $25 million;
2 managing the continuing business;
3 preparing action plans and presentations.

The success depends upon the quality of the management and the credibility of their plans. If there has been regular and clear communication throughout, then it is more likely that they will succeed. At one level further on, control may be removed from them by either lenders or shareholders if they are not successful. In the final analysis, lenders and shareholders can decide that enough is enough and the group may fold.

What is clear is that a senior member of management must always be aware of the key factors that ensure continuing liquidity and maintain the external relationships with those who provide it.

D and L Engineering

This is a small business with one employee other than the owner, serving the offshore oil industry and local agricultural community in north-east Scotland. It was established with the proprietor's capital of £20,000 and bank loans and overdraft of the same amount together with a regional interest-free loan to purchase machines of £10,000 from the local development agency. This is to be repaid in monthly instalments starting in 18 months.

The first 6 months of the business were involved in setting-up the workshop and developing the necessary business contacts. A number of regular orders were obtained and the major customers accounted for the following proportions of the work: A 60%; B 20%; C 5%. The balance of orders were from local farmers, but an increasing reputation for prompt and high-quality work means that this area is growing. There is little time to seek new contracts as existing customers more than occupy current capacity, even though this might be desirable to diversify the customer base.

Liquidity Management in Practice

The first full year's turnover was £80,000 and there was a healthy profit of £25,000. Drawings had not been high, yet the overdraft limit of £10,000 was often close to being exceeded. There was a need to expand the business by buying new machines costing £15,000 and by employing another engineer in order to take some pressure off the existing staff. This would leave seven machines between the three of them.

A closer examination of the past 3 months' figures is given in table 8.4. In order to buy the new machine, the owner decided to approach his bank for a further loan. The initial reaction from the bank was that it wished to continue to support this business but that it would need clear projections for the coming year and also seek a steady reduction of the overdraft.

This prompted a detailed analysis of the current position in order to establish the next few months. In particular, the working capital position needed examination. In order to support him, the owner employed an accountant for a few hours to carry out the analysis.

On the assumption that the proportions of work carried out for A and B were correct, then total receipts in the last 3 months from A should have been around £12,000 and from B around £4000. However, the actual figures were £6900 and

Table 8.4 D and L Engineering: past 3 months' figures

	Month 1	Month 2	Month 3
Sales	6500	6250	7150
Receipts from A	3000	2900	1000
Receipts from B		1000	
New machines	2500		

£1000 respectively. Clearly, both these areas warranted further examination. A detailed analysis revealed:

- A took 30 days' credit provided that the invoices were submitted by the end of the month, otherwise they would have to wait until the end of the following month.
- The owner had failed to submit invoices totalling £5000 to A due to pressure of work.
- B took erratic periods of credit, but there were £3000 of invoices more than 45 days past due.
- A complete analysis of all sales and invoices showed that there were more than £10,000 of invoices either not submitted or overdue (i.e. over 30 days).

Thus, £10,000 could be raised from sorting out the debtor position alone. This would ensure the complete removal of the overdraft. A further analysis showed that the current level of profitability would pay for the machine in a little over 5 months within the current overdraft.

There also needed to be an analysis of the other components of working capital. D and L held little stock, which tended only to be bought in as needed, therefore this was unlikely to be a problem. However, D and L had always prided itself on paying its bills on time. This meant in practice that bills were paid weekly. If D and L moved on to taking 21 days' credit, this would release a further £1500 into the business.

The simple pressures of day-to-day business had meant that a lack of control could have led to unnecessary financial pressures. The introduction of a monthly financial review would allow adequate control of working capital as well as a better analysis of the business, including costing of individual jobs and identification of the most profitable business.

Liquidity Management in Practice

Megacorp

This is a diversified multinational corporation based in the USA with a market capitalization of $5 billion. It is about to launch a bid for Target PLC for £2.5 billion. The acquisition will be financed by debt denominated in sterling and which will be repaid by a mixture of asset disposals and operating cash flow. It has been decided to manage the currency exposure from the potential acquisition by borrowing in sterling from a banking syndicate. There is the possibility of raising fresh equity if need be.

There are a number of liquidity management issues which arise from this acquisition:

1 Megacorp is exposed to rising sterling interest rates. It will not wish to draw down the loans before it actually has to pay for Target. Indeed the acquisition may not proceed. In this case, it could protect itself against this risk by taking out options on sterling interest rates. Further, because the size of the acquisition is so large, it may also wish to purchase 'swaptions' (options on swaps) so that it can decide to fix a large element of the potential sterling debt.
2 If the acquisition proceeds, it will want to be able to use any free cash within Target as well as its operating cash flow. Therefore, it must have ready systems to allow it to:
(a) obtain reliable cash forecasts promptly after acquisition;
(b) net surplus cash within Target against borrowings within the rest of Megacorp;
(c) impose daily cash reporting of balances within Target;
(d) establish intra-group payment systems in order to limit bank charges;
(e) impose deposit policies and limits;
(f) renegotiate borrowing facilities;
(g) identify and sell any peripheral assets in Target.

Liquidity Management in Practice

In reality, these are the same controls and systems that any business of whatever size would need, but without the day-to-day operational controls, which a company the size of Target should have in any case. The basic principles would remain the same, even though the companies operate in different countries. Local money transmission rules and banking systems and instruments may differ, but the basic issues of:

- cash flow information;
- analysing that information;
- selecting appropriate instruments;
- managing interest periods and risk;

will be the same the whole world over. In the final analysis, ensuring the availability of cash to meet liabilities will be the first objective of both liquidity and treasury management.

9
Organizing Liquidity Management

- Setting authorities for the organization of liquidity management

For many small businesses not all the techniques described in this book will be applicable, and similarly staffing may well be carried out as part of the duties of the bookkeeper or accountant. However, the basic principles can be followed by businesses of whatever size.

For larger companies, and certainly for large multinational groups, the business of liquidity management normally forms part of the treasury department which ought to have suitably experienced and qualified staff. For all companies there will need to be an agreement on how the staff are to be monitored and evaluated and also how much delegated decision-taking will take place. While the day-to-day business of money transmission and managing short-term depositing and borrowing should be capable of being left in the hands of operational staff, policy decisions about deposit limits and interest rate policy need to be reviewed and approved by at least the finance director and, ideally, by a suitable board subcommittee.

Organizing Liquidity Management

These instructions should set out the limits within which specified members of staff may operate and how exceptions are to be approved. The initial judgement by the board (or whoever that judgement is delegated to) needs to be taken after careful consideration of the risks involved – after all, if the policy is complied with and something goes wrong, the board will need to recognize their own involvement. Typically, the initial proposal might be made by the treasurer – so that is where the greatest responsibility lies.

A typical initial approval might include the following aspects:

Deposit policy

Deposits may only be placed with the following institutions and totals outstanding with each may not exceed the amount specified:

- £20 million: A, B, C, D.
- £10 million: E, F, G, H.
- £5 million: I, J.
- £1 million: K,L,M,N,P,R,S,T.

Additionally commercial paper may be purchased for periods of up to 1 month with a limit of £5 million for any one group of companies and with a maximum maturity of 1 month provided that the issuer (or guarantor) has a rating of at least A1, P1.

Deposits in excess of 6 months must be approved by the finance director and in excess of 1 year by the treasury committee.

Interest rate

- It is the general policy that $x\%$ of borrowings greater than 1 year should be at fixed interest rates.
- Interest rate options which do not reflect an underlying borrowing or deposit requirement must not be bought or sold.
- Detailed management of interest rate risk less than 1 year is delegated to the treasury committee.

(Note: the policy would also extend to more detailed funding management and also to detailed policy on currency management.)

Putting Liquidity into Practice

References are made above to a treasury committee. It is a matter of individual judgement as to how much policy should be reserved to the committee and how much delegated to the treasurer and his or her staff. In practice, the art of deciding what is going to happen to interest rates over the next few months and also to interpreting internal forecasts is often taken by consensus between colleagues, and the forum of a treasury committee allows broad policy to be formed while the specialist dealers and other staff are able to make the more short-term judgements.

Membership of the committee

It will be a matter of style and the size of the group as to whether or not this is a formal subcommittee of the board

Organizing Liquidity Management

(rather like the audit committee). If it is a subcommittee, then it will probably be composed entirely of directors with the treasurer and possibly his or her deputy in attendance.

Often, a more practical forum is to bring together individuals who are conversant with the techniques and instruments involved, but who may not necessarily be involved in direct treasury management. In this case, the finance director and the financial controller together with the treasurer (plus deputy, probably) might be joined by other non-financial staff with a view to reaching balanced judgements. In particular, the assessment of risk may make someone like the company secretary a useful participant.

Agenda

A typical agenda might include the following.

Review of action since the last meeting

This could cover the actual outturn compared to expectations of decisions taken at previous meetings. There could also be a review of actual interest costs compared with given market indicators, such as average 3-month LIBOR.

Examination of cash flow forecasts

In addition to a balanced discussion of future funding or deposit arrangements, the committee can consider the sensitivities of the cash flow and may spot errors or risks that had been missed. This type of discussion allows a spreading of risk in terms of decision-making – it is unwise to rely entirely on the judgement of one individual.

Review of economic indicators

Perhaps quarterly, the committee should review the major economic forecasts for the economies in which the group operates. This might take the form of a summary of certain bank economist forecasts, giving a range of views on future interest rates and currency rates. The committee could then come to its own view on what might happen to rates. As discussed in chapter 4, the company needs to come to its own view on rates before it can decide whether any hedging needs to take place.

As an alternative to a summary of bank forecasts, the company might employ a specific forecasting service who would create reports specifically for the company.

Short-term interest rates

In practice, decisions about interest rates up to 6 months may be delegated to operational staff, but the combination of the cash flow forecasts and the committee's views on future interest rates can provide some direction on whether to keep rates short or long and how much protection through the use of hedging instruments needs to be taken out.

Long-term interest rates

If appropriate, the committee may take decisions (or make recommendations to the board) about the structure of long-term interest rates.

Organizing Liquidity Management

Frequency

Meetings might be held monthly, or for less complex groups, perhaps quarterly. In the meantime it must be clear who is responsible for reviewing the position and how decisions can be taken between meetings. In practice, the treasurer (or appropriate subordinate for large groups) will review the detailed position on a weekly basis.

Style of Company

The precise way of operating will depend greatly upon the style and culture of the organization. Many decentralized companies have very small central treasuries. The scope for managing liquidity will therefore depend upon how much responsibility is left with the operating units. Companies may decide that decisions even about risk should be left at the operating unit, otherwise the entrepreneurial spirit will be diminished. Banks, however, like to have a central point of contact – this may end up being the finance director in a small head office.

For companies with strong central financial controls and for small businesses, the precise method of operation will need to suit the company as the company, in the end, has its own cash cycle and, therefore, liquidity needs.

Glossary

Acceptance credit: a short-term financing facility under which the borrower draws bills of exchange on a bank which accepts them and discounts them in the market to provide cash for the borrower.

Arbitrage: operating simultaneously in two different, but mutually relevant, markets so as to profit from a temporary misalignment between them.

At the money: used to describe an option where the strike price is the same as the underlying commodity.

Bank float: time spent by a remittance in the banking system during which its amount is available to neither the payer nor the payee.

Bank transfer: a remittance process whereby a payer makes a payment at any branch of any bank for the account of a payee at any branch of the same or other bank. Also called credit transfer or direct transfer.

Banker's payment: payment order issued by a bank on behalf of its customer, whereby the recipient looks to the bank for settlement, thus minimizing credit risk. Also called a banker's draft.

Glossary

Base rate: basic lending rate of a bank or financial institution in the UK. Used as the reference rate for overdraft lending.

Basic cover (Export Credits Guarantee Department) (ECGD): the basic credit insurance guarantee or policy, i.e. the comprehensive guarantee, the supplemental extended terms guarantee or the specific guarantee.

Basis: the price difference between a financial futures contract and its underlying contract.

Basis point: 1/100th of 1%, i.e. 0.01%.

Bid–offer spread: the difference between two rates at which a bank is willing to borrow and lend funds or to buy and sell a currency or other financial instrument: the difference represents its dealing margin.

Bill of exchange: an unconditional order in writing addressed by one person (the drawer) to another, signed by the person giving it, requiring the person to whom it is addressed to pay on demand, or at a fixed or determinable future time, a sum certain in money, to or to the order of, a specified person or to bearer.

Bond (security): an interest-bearing certificate of debt, usually for a term of 5 years or more, executed under seal.

Certificate of deposit (CD): evidence of a deposit with a specified bank or building society repayable on a fixed date. They are negotiable instruments and in the UK they have a secondary market.

Cleared balance: balance on a bank account excluding any receipts which do not yet represent cleared value.

Cleared value: the time at which a credit to a customer's bank account becomes fully available to the customer, and effective for calculating interest and for establishing the undrawn balance of a facility (if overdrawn).

Clearing: the process by which a payment through the banking system is transferred from the payer's to the payee's account.

Glossary

Clearing house: an organization guaranteeing settlement of trades on a futures exchange.

Collection account: a bank account opened for the specific purpose of speeding up the receipt of cleared value for remittances from specific customers or groups of customers, usually at a distant or foreign location or in a foreign currency. In the USA called a 'lockbox'.

Commercial credit risk: the risk that a customer will not pay on time, due to its insolvency or other causes specific to the customer rather than to its country or currency.

Commercial paper: unsecured promissory notes.

Commitment fee: a percentage per annum charged by a lender on the daily balance of a borrowing facility, usually charged on the undrawn balance of the facility.

Confirmed irrevocable letter of credit (CILC): an irrevocable letter of credit not merely notified but also confirmed to the payee by a bank usually in its own country, which amounts to a guarantee of payment by that bank so long as the payee complies with the terms of the credit. (Note that if the bank is not in a creditworthy country, there may be foreign exchange control problems.)

Confiscation risk: the risk that assets in a foreign country may be confiscated, expropriated or nationalized, or that the distant owner's control may be interfered with.

Correspondent bank: a bank in one country which, when so required, acts as an agent for a bank in another country, typically formalized by the holding of reciprocal bank accounts.

Country cheques: any cheques which are not town cheques and go through the general as opposed to the town clearing.

Depth of market: an indication of the volume of interest by both buyers and sellers. The opposite of a 'thin market'.

Direct transfer: see bank transfer.

Glossary

Eligible bills: acceptance credits drawn subject to the Bank of England's rules on eligibility and accepted by certain banks whose acceptances are eligible for rediscount at the finest rates at the Bank of England.

Euro– (banks, currency, deposit, dollar, sterling, bond): a Eurocurrency deposit is a deposit in a bank account located outside the banking regulations of the country which issues the currency. Thus a Eurodollar deposit is a US dollar deposit held outside the USA or in an international banking facility in the USA. The prefix 'Euro' is often synonymous with 'offshore'.

Factoring: buying invoiced debts, and taking responsibility from the seller for sales accounting and debt collection.

Financial futures: contracts for the delivery at a future date of specified financial instruments or currency deposits; such contracts, like commodity futures, are traded in formal, open-outcry markets.

Float: see bank float.

Floating rate note (FRN): bonds on which the rate of interest is established periodically by reference to short-term interest rates.

Forfaiting: acceptance by a bank (forfaitor) of medium– or long-term bills of exchange without recourse to the seller.

Forward forward: a contract with a bank for a term borrowing or deposit to commence at a stated future date but at a rate specified at the time of the contract.

Futures: contracts for the delivery at a future date of standard amounts of a commodity, or a financial instrument or of a currency; such contracts are traded in formal, open-outcry markets.

Gilt-edged securities: British government stocks.

Hedge: to take action to protect the business against price fluctuations, usually in exchange or interest rates.

Glossary

Irrevocable letter of credit: a letter of credit which cannot be cancelled by the payer or its bank which issued the letter of credit.

Inter-bank: any transaction between banks, including deposits by one bank with another in the inter-bank market at interbank bid and offer rates, i.e. the rates at which a bank is willing to accept or make such deposits respectively.

Interest rate exposure: the cost to the business of changes in interest rates.

Invoice discounting: a commercial creditor sells its invoices to a factor (see factoring) at a discount for immediate cash; invoice discounting does not include sales accounting and debt collecting. The creditor still has to collect the debt for the factor.

Issuing and paying agent: a bank or other party which holds the notes (e.g. commercial paper) on behalf of a borrower until required to be issued and which handles the payments on issue and maturity of the notes.

Letter of credit: a formal undertaking by an importer's bank at the importer's request and in accordance with the importer's instructions either to pay, negotiate or accept bills of exchange drawn by the exporter or to authorize another bank to do this, against specific documents, provided that the terms of the credit are complied with. Such a credit can be revocable or irrevocable.

LIBID: London inter-bank bid rate.

LIBOR: London inter-bank offered rate. The rate at which banks will lend funds to another bank of similar creditworthiness.

Liquid (instrument): one which the purchaser is readily able to sell before maturity.

Long position: assets exceed liabilities in given commodity. The opposite of a short position.

Glossary

Mandate: authority given to a bank to open an account, defining the way in which it is to be operated.

Margin: (a) difference between buying and selling price; (b) the change in value in a contract traded on a futures exchange which has to be matched with a cash deposit. Also the initial deposit made when purchasing the contract.

Maturity: the date at which a debt or other payments fall due.

Maturity structure: the pattern of maturities among the assets and liabilities of the business.

Money-market: consists of financial institutions and dealers in money and credit; in the UK the Bank of England, the deposit banks and the discount and accepting houses.

Multiple option facility (MOF): a credit facility allowing the borrower to determine the borrowing instrument, interest rate period, amount and currency, without prejudicing the total amount available over an agreed term.

Negotiable instrument: any financial instrument like bills of exchange, promissory notes, cheques, banknotes, CDs, share warrants, or bearer shares or debentures, the title of which passes without notice to the person liable on the instrument and in which a transferee in good faith and for a consideration of value acquires an indefeasible title.

Option: the right, but not the obligation, to buy (call) or sell (put) a commodity.

Option, American: an option which may be exercised at any time prior to expiration.

Option, call: the right to buy a commodity.

Option, European: an option which may only be exercised on its expiration date.

Option, put: the right to sell a commodity.

Revolving limits: a limit of a borrowing facility which permits the reborrowing of amounts repaid, and restricts the total outstanding balance.

Glossary

Sales mix: the proportions of business sales with different operating characteristics like gross margins, so that a change in these proportions would change the overall performance of the business.

Secondary market: a market in financial instruments after their issue, which improves the liquidity of the holders of those instruments.

Short deposits: current accounts, overnight deposits and money at call; deposits with longer maturities are term deposits.

Spread: see bid–offer spread.

Stop loss: an order to sell a financial instrument when its price falls to a specified level.

Tender panel: a group of banks tendering competitively to lend money.

Tender panel agent: co-ordinates tender panel bids and interfaces with the borrower.

Tenor = usance: the period for which a bill of exchange or promissory note is expressed to run to maturity; a tenor bill contrasts with a sight bill which is payable on sight.

Term deposit, time deposit: deposits, including CDs, for periods longer than sight deposits.

Thin market: see depth of market.

Town cheques, town clearing: cheques for £10,000 or more and drawn on accounts within the City of London and paid into other such accounts, are cleared within the same day, whereas all other cheques go into the general clearing and take 2 days or more to clear.

Value, value date: the point in time when a bank remittance actually becomes available to the payee for use.

Appendix 1
Useful Calculations

Note: where x is the rate to be converted and y is the revised rate.

To semi-annualize an annual rate x

$$y = \left(\sqrt{\frac{x}{100} + 1} \right) - 1 \times 200$$

To make an annual rate x into quarterly rate y

$$y = \left(\sqrt[4]{\frac{x}{100} + 1} \right) - 1 \times 400$$

To annualize a semi-annual rate x

$$y = \left(\frac{x}{200} + 1 \right)^2 - 1 \times 100$$

Appendix 1 Useful Calculations

To annualize a quarterly rate x

$$y = \left(\frac{x}{400} + 1\right)^4 - 1 \times 100$$

To semiannualize a quarterly rate x

$$y = \left(\frac{x}{400} + 1\right)^2 - 1 \times 200$$

True yield basis of y from a given discount rate x

For a 365-day year basis and for a discount period of d days

$$y = \frac{36{,}500x}{36{,}500 - xd}$$

Appendix 2 Sample ACT Examination Questions

This appendix provides specimen answers to questions which have been set as part of the Association of Corporate Treasurers' examinations in liquidity management between 1987 and 1991. The particular questions have been selected because of their relevance to the breadth of the subject and in particular how liquidity is applied in practice. The examination questions are often set with no single correct answer for the discussion questions. Therefore, it is often difficult to say that the suggested answer is a complete or correct answer for that question or that this would represent the standard expected in an examination. However, the purpose of providing the specimen answers (which are the author's own) is to try to show the thought process required in dealing with the consequences of liquidity management.

Question 1 (1990)

Robins PLC is a company which manufactures computerized manufacturing systems. It has accepted a contract from

Appendix 2 ACT Examination Questions

Modern Manufacturing Systems PLC (MMS) to supply an integrated manufacturing system to a new factory which MMS is building. The contract represents a substantial share of Robins' business for the current year.

Base rates are currently 12% (1 September 1988) and Robins finances itself from overdrafts, except for a fully drawn term facility at 13% p.a. of £2 million which expires on 31 December 1989.

The price for the contract has been agreed with MMS at £2.0 million and MMS will pay 50% of the contract price on 30 November 1988 and the balance on 28 February 1989.

The contract begins on 1 September 1988 and runs for 6 months. In order to fulfil the contract Robins purchased components on 1 September for £1.6 million. This purchase was for cash and will be followed by four successive monthly payments of £50,000 by Robins to cover installation costs for the system. The first of these payments takes place on 1 November 1988. MMS has agreed to reimburse Robins in full in addition for installation costs 1 month after they are incurred.

Robins has been experiencing difficulties in its working capital management over the last 2 years; its overdraft has risen sharply and as at 1 September 1988 stood at £4 million. Its bank requires it to fall to £3.5 million by 31 March 1989 and not to increase in the meantime. Robins' treasurer has proposed the following as the means of financing the working capital requirements of the MMS contract:

1 Robins will increase the credit taken from suppliers for the normal business from its usual 2 months to 3 months, beginning with certain invoices which would have been due for settlement at the end of each of the 3 months from 30 September and to attempt to maintain this lag thereafter. Each month's invoices which are to be delayed are worth £800,000. The cost of this additional credit is the loss of

Appendix 2 ACT Examination Questions

discounts worth £40,000 per month starting with October's discounts.
2. Robins will reduce its orders for stocks by £100,000 per month for the first 3 months of the contract. Destocking will take the form of reduced orders for raw materials and components placed with suppliers. Stocks are planned to be returned to their established levels by an order for £300,000 for raw materials and components placed on 31 December 1988.
3. Robins will factor trade debtors worth £2.1 million on 1 September. The factor will take a fee of 5% of the debts factored and will pay 90% of the value of the debtors to Robins on 1 September and the remaining 5% on 1 October. The debts factored represent 3 months' sales at £700,000 per month and would normally have been paid in equal instalments on 1 October, 1 November and 1 December.

It is to be assumed that, apart from the MMS contract, Robins would be able to work within its existing facilities.

Required

(a) Forecast the monthly cash flows resulting from the MMS contract based on the information given above.
(b) Draft a report to the treasurer of Robins on the liquidity management implications of the MMS contract. Your report should include suggestions on management policy and should refer to the advantages and limitations of the methods being suggested for financing the working capital requirements of the contract as well as other points which you consider relevant.
(c) Explain briefly the alternative methods available for forecasting the liquidity of a company such as Robins, identifying the advantages and disadvantages of each and commenting on the main information requirements. In particular, discuss the sources of uncertainty in this forecast.

Appendix 2 ACT Examination Questions

(d) Set out the interest rate risks which Robins faces and put these in the context of its business risks. How might the treasurer of Robins manage these?

Answer to question 1

(a)

The cash forecast (table A2.1) is prepared by a standard receipts and payments method. The technique is to identify the differences that arise from the contract. In particular, because factoring has been used to accelerate payments, the normal cash flow has to be deducted later on.

Table A2.1 Cash flow forecast for MMS contract (£000)

	1/9/88	1/10/88	1/11/88	1/12/88	1/1/89	1/2/89	1/3/89
Contract price				1000			1000
Components	(1600)						
Installation costs			(50)	(50)	(50)	(50)	
reimbursement				50	50	50	50
Reduction in stock			100	100	100		
Restocking							(300)
Receipt from factor	1890	105					
Lost cash flow from debtors			(700)	(700)	(700)		
Delays in payments to creditors		800					
Lost discount			(40)	(40)	(40)	(40)	(40)
Net cash flow	290	205	(690)	360	60	(40)	710
Overdraft	(4000) (3710)	(3505)	(4195)	(3835)	(3775)	(3815)	(3105)

134

Appendix 2 ACT Examination Questions

Analysis of cash flow

Contract	400
Factor	(105)
Creditors	600
	895

Cash flow assumptions

1 *Contract price*: Dates given (30 Nov. = 1 Dec.; 28 Feb. = 1 March).
2 *Components*: Initial purchase of £1.6 million given at 1.9.88.
3 *Installation*: Given as commencing 1.11.88 (with 1 month stagger for reimbursements).
4 *Creditors*: Delay invoices worth £800,000 starting at 30.9.88 (=1.10.88); 1 month stagger; loss of discount of £40,000 associated with payments of creditors with 1 month's delay.

Excludes interest charges.

(b)

- The contract places considerable strain on Robins. The overdraft limit of £4 million is breached in November (and there may be other breaches as we do not have mid-month data) and if there are any delays, the target of £3.6 million by 31 March may be ambitious.
- The net cash flow from the contract is £400,000 (before interest), but this is at the cost of the cash outflow of £150,000 to the factor. In effect the overdraft target is being met by a one-time delay in payments to creditors.
- The gross margin on the contract is only 20% (i.e. before overheads) – this will be reduced further if computed on a discounted cash flow (DCF) basis.

Appendix 2 ACT Examination Questions

- The significant cash flow advantages arise from manipulation of working capital – should these not have been available in any case? The delay in payments to creditors could have been delayed were it not for the MMS contract.
- Could reduced stock levels be maintained after the end of the contract. In the meantime, will this cause lost business?
- Factoring is fairly expensive. Stretching creditors is again expensive, but there is the risk of a knock-on effect of causing other creditors to accelerate payments due to credit concern.

Overall, the *contract* consumes capital for what may be a low return and putting strain on the cash flow. If there are delays or if payments due become bad debts, this will cause further problems for Robins. In any case the bank's overdraft requirements are not met. What will this cause the bank to do? Are there any fall-back positions?

(c)

(The first half of this part calls for a restatement of the principles behind the receipts and payments method and the source and application method as set out in chapter 2.)

The sources of uncertainty in this forecast:

- errors in forecasting cost and duration of the contract;
- control delays in receipts (note Robins's controls costs);
- bad debts;
- pressure from creditors;
- business downturn.

(d)

1 The principal interest rate risk arises from an exposure to floating interest rates on the overdraft.

Appendix 2 ACT Examination Questions

2 Significantly, an increase in interest rates will aggravate the cash-limit problem.
3 There is a further risk arising from the need to refinance the fixed rate loan at the end of 1989.
4 The business risks are significant in that Robins cannot afford to take risks with interest rates and therefore it is desirable to fix rates wherever possible. These might be achieved by:
   (a) agreeing to borrow for 3 or 6 months fixed (whether directly from the clearing bank or another bank);
   (b) purchasing a base rate option;
   (c) buying an FRA for (say) the period January–March.
   It may not be sensible on cost grounds (or possible on credit grounds) to protect the refinancing risk at December 1989 until the position is clearer after March 1989.
5 Other business risks include:
   (a) technological risk;
   (b) economic downturn;
   (c) level of competition;
   (d) pressure from creditors;
   (e) cancellation of orders.

Other measures to be taken include:

- close monitoring of receipts;
- tight control of work-in-progress;
- close monitoring of creditor reaction to longer payment terms.

Specifically, tight cash forecasting and reporting.

Question 2 (1991)

Conglomerate PLC is the holding company of a group of companies. The operating portion of the group in the UK

Appendix 2 ACT Examination Questions

consists of three wholly owned subsidiaries, Sellit Ltd, Makeit Ltd and Developit Ltd. Sellit is a chain of supermarkets with national coverage; Makeit manufactures building materials; and Developit is a property development company specializing in major office developments.

In table A2.2 are extracts from the balance sheets of the three group companies. For each of the companies data are given for the financial year just ended and from the budgeted balance sheets for the coming year.

In table A2.3 is data derived from the budgeted profit and loss accounts of the three companies for the coming year.

Turnover in the year ended 31.8.91 was as follows Sellit £2536 million, Makeit £3392 million and Developit £370 million.

The capital budgets of the three companies for the year are summarized in table A2.4.

The budgeted financial information has been prepared on assumptions about the operations of the three companies and the market conditions in which they are expected to operate. Sellit has been assumed to continue to increase its market share in a very competitive retailing market while continuing to reduce unit costs and increase its net profit margins. Developit's profits depend cruicially upon the sale of a large office development. Negotiations for its sale are at an advanced stage but have been stalled and there is doubt about whether the sale will be completed.

Sellit's operating cash flows arise regularly through the year. Its capital expenditure plans for the coming year are part of a programme of new store development begun some years ago and which is expected to continue for several more years. Makeit's capital expenditure programme for the coming year is expected to be at its height during autumn/winter 1991/92. Developit's expected cash flows are dominated by the planned sale of the major office development referred to

Table A2.2 Selected balance sheet data for Group companies, year ended 31.8.91 and budgeted for the year to 31.8.92 (£ million)

	Sellit		Makeit		Developit	
	Year ended 31.8.91	Budget to 31.8.92	Year ended 31.8.91	Budget to 31.8.92	Year ended 31.8.91	Budget to 31.8.92
Fixed assets	1416	1617	1205	1265	982	989
Current assets						
Stock	179	192	392	499	108	173
Debtors	49	39	500	535	25	55
Cash	27	79	89	72	2	5
Creditors of less than 1 year						
Overdrafts	59	2	116	116	6	9
Trade	286	332	131	146	30	30
Taxation	45	69	105	43	9	2
Other (excluding provisions)	53	100	17	24	4	4
Provisions	40	50	22	30	1	1

above. If the sale goes ahead it will occur towards the end of the company's accounting year.

The three companies each have substantial bank borrowings in addition to the overdrafts indicated in table A2.2. Their borrowings at 31.8.91 were: Sellit £213 million, Makeit £421 million and Developit £550 million. Of Developit's borrowings, £300 million are fixed-rate and project-specific. Sellit's loan facilities have recently been renegotiated for the coming year, while those of Makeit are due for renegotiation in November 1991 and those of Developit which are not project-related are due for renegotiation in April 1992.

Appendix 2 ACT Examination Questions

Table A2.3 Budgeted profit and loss account data for the year to 31.8.92 (£ million)

	Sellit	*Makeit*	*Developit*
Turnover	2984	3571	533
Profit after interest and tax	185	250	80
Depreciation	69	117	30
Provisions for future redundancy expenses	13	5	—
Profit on disposal of fixed assets	5	20	13
Interest costs charged to profit and loss	39	85	30
Interest costs capitalized	31	—	15
Interest received	41	16	5
Taxation charged for the year	40	30	5

Table A2.4 Summary capital budgets of UK operating companies (£ million)

	Sellit	*Makeit*	*Developit*
Capital expenditure	385	257	55
Disposals of fixed assets (at net book value)	115	80	18

Required

(a) Forecast the annual cash flows of Sellit, Makeit and Developit for the year ending 31.8.92.

(b) Comment on the cash flows of each of the three group companies and their resulting consequences for the liquidity management in the group overall, taking care to identify any uncertainties and risks.

Appendix 2 ACT Examination Questions

Answer to question 2

(a)
Answer is given in table A2.5.

Table A2.5 Cash flow forecasts for the three companies for the year ending 31.8.92 (£ million)

	Sellit	Makeit	Developit
Profit	185	250	80
+ Depreciation	69	117	30
Provisions	13	5	—
Capitalized interest	(31)	—	(15)
	236	372	95
Less profit on disposal of fixed assets	(5)	(20)	(13)
Adjusted cash flow	231	352	82
Stocks	(13)	(107)	(65)
Debtors	10	(35)	(30)
Creditors	46	15	—
Tax paid	(16)	(92)	(12)
Operating cash flow	258	133	(25)
Capex. (less interest capitalized)	(354)	(257)	(40)
Disposal of fixed assets	120	100	31
Other creditors	47	7	—
Provisions	(3)	3	—
	68	(14)	(34)
Increase in overdraft	(57)	—	3
Decrease in cash	(52)	17	(3)
Therefore, reduction in other borrowings	(41)	3	(34)

Appendix 2 ACT Examination Questions

	Sellit	Makeit	Developit
Borrowings at 31.8.91	213	421	550
Budgeted other debt at 31.8.92	254	418	584
Fixed asset reconciliation			
Opening FA	1416	1205	982
+ Capex	385	257	55
− Depreciation	(69)	(117)	(30)
− Book value of assets sold	(115)	(80)	(18)
Closing FA	1617	1265	989
Tax payment			
Opening balance	45	105	9
Charge to P&L	40	30	5
Closing balance	(69)	(43)	(2)
Therefore, cash payment	16	92	12

(b)
First, some basic ratios are helpful in considering the working capital movements for each division (table A2.6).

Table A2.6 Basic ratios

	Sellit (%)	Makeit (%)	Developit (%)
Sales growth	17.7	5.3	44.1
Stock growth	7.3	27.3	60.2
Debtors' growth	(20.4)	7.0	120.0
Creditors' growth	16.1	11.5	—
Net working capital movement	(74.1)	16.7	92.2

Appendix 2 ACT Examination Questions

Significant points are:

- Across the group only Sellit is generating cash despite having the largest capex programme. In total only £20 million will be generated – will this be enough to service group dividends, debt service and other requirements?

Looking at each division:

1 Sellit:
   (a) The operating cash flow does not cover capex and this will be dependent upon the ability to sell fixed assets. If the prices anticipated cannot be realized, can/will capex be restricted?
   (b) Continuing use of creditors as a source of capital – this increases broadly in line with sales.
   (c) One-off redirection in the level of debtors. These are small in amount and the redirection will not be sustainable.
2 Makeit:
   (a) Modest sales growth, but high increases in working capital, particularly stock. Will stock be saleable if market turns? Are these stocks necessary?
   (b) Again capex is not covered by operating cash flow. Capex occurs early in the year and therefore if profits do not reach budgeted levels, the cash position may be considerably worse at year-end.
   (c) Similar concerns as for Sellit arise about the achievability of asset sales.
3 Developit:
   (a) Clearly working capital is increasing at too high a rate. The increase in debtors may represent the anticipated sale before the year-end, with cash to be received after 31.8.92.
   (b) Stocks may represent an increasing level of properties for resale. Care may need to be exercised if these assets are not funded on a non-recourse basis.

Appendix 2 ACT Examination Questions

(c) Approaching 50% of Developit's borrowing are at variable interest rates with consequent risks in a notoriously volatile business. This represents a significant risk.

(d) The possibility of a delay in the sale of the office development is clearly a major risk.

Group implications

- At the operating level, the group depends on Sellit's cash flow, although Makeit would be more important if its stocks could be better controlled.
- There is no obvious cash generation to finance the expansion of the other divisions. This could not continue indefinitely.
- The divisions operate in industries with different risk profiles. Financing Developit would be easier if the group were prepared to allow offset and cross-guarantee arrangements. The group will need to consider carefully its corporate ethics and balance this against the desire to make the divisions self-supporting.
- Similarly, does the group want to optimize interest costs by operating a netting arrangement? The seasonality of the business may assist this.
- The group is generally skewed towards cash generation in the second half; this has obvious risks.
- There are a range of uncertainties in the budgeting process which can be mitigated by keeping tight cash controls. In particular, the expectations of rising sales and falling margins which may be beaten by competitive pressures.
- Makeit has a higher level of overdraft funding compared to the other divisions. It may be sensible to increase the level of Sellit's overdraft, but increase committed borrowings within Makeit.
- Why do divisions negotiate annually? It would be more sensible to take a medium-term group view.
- There will be a need to ensure a 'safe' level of facilities in the event of a downturn.

(Note: there are further points which could be made, but these seem to me to be the major issues that an examination candidate could be expected to raise.)

Question 3 (1987)

Your company is a medium-sized manufacturer of consumer goods which are sold direct to small retail organizations. There are no particularly large customers, and your sales exhibit virtually no seasonality.

It is 10 days before your year-end for 'this year'; information is provided for 'last year', an estimate based on the last forecast from the accounts department for 'this year' and an estimate for 'next year'.

(a) What is the appropriate method for determining now the cash balance:
   (i) at 'this year's' balance sheet date?
   (ii) one month after 'this year's' balance sheet date?
(b) If your current overdraft limit is agreed at £18 million and is fully utilized approximately once every 2 months:
   (i) Calculate any change in credit facilities required for next year.
   (ii) What form should the change in facilities take?
   (iii) How would you ensure the efficient monitoring and control of the working capital investment?

Financial information is given in table A2.7.

Appendix 2 ACT Examination Questions

Table A2.7 Financial information (£ million)

	Last year	This year	Next year
Sales	70	100	140
Profit before tax[a]	14	20	30
Year-end working capital[b]	21	30	42
Capital expenditure	3	10	28
Tax paid	3	4	7
Dividends paid	3	4	7

[a] PBT stated after charging depreciation: £4 million (last year); £4 million (this year); £7 million (next year).
[b] Year-end working capital is defined as the absolute value of 'stock+debtors−creditors', not the change in these values.

Answer to question 3

(a)(i)
The receipts and payments method would be the normal method for such a short period. This will allow close identification of individual items, particularly large sums.

Care will need to be exercised as payments may be erratic around balance sheet date.

Daily monitoring will be required to observe any significant variations.

(a)(ii)
The extension of the time period to 40 days is still likely to mean that the receipts and payments method is appropriate.

Appendix 2 ACT Examination Questions

The important consideration is whether the cashier is in a position to predict the flows from debtors and to creditors over the period.

Again, care will need to be taken over any 'unusual' adjustments around year-end.

(b)(i)
Cash flow for next year will be (£ million):

Profit	30
+ Depreciation	7
− Working capital	(12)
− Tax paid	(7)
− Dividends paid	(7)
− Capital expenditure	(28)
	(17)

Therefore the additional requirement will be £17 million, although we have not been given information on movements within the year; e.g. early capital expenditure, tax or dividends.

The total requirements may, therefore, be higher.

(b)(ii)
What is the extra funding for? It could be argued to be for capital expenditure or working capital – in either case the funding seems to be becoming permanent. Certainly, the funding should be more certain than overdraft – therefore term or committed debt seems appropriate (although a weak balance sheet might call for equity).

Appendix 2 ACT Examination Questions

The additional cost of term debt needs to be evaluated.

(b)(iii)

- Separate reporting and control should be undertaken for debtors, stock and creditors.
- Ageing of debtors to look for slow progress and possible bad debts.
- Stock levels should be identified by department so that work-in-progress and high levels of raw materials can be controlled.
- Appropriate discounts from creditors should be taken, with appropriate procedures to control timing of payments.

Regular sales reporting will also allow early warning of opportunities to cut (or indeed, the need to increase) stocks.

Question 4 (1989)

Speculative PLC is a company whose main activity is the manufacture of taps and drills for the engineering industry. The treasury department of Speculative is preparing an analysis of the company's liquidity. The company's overdraft at the beginning of the present financial year 1 July 1988, was £3,545,255. Speculative has agreed with its bankers that the overdraft facility be reduced to £2.2 million from 30 June 1990.

Table A2.8 reproduces Speculative's profit and loss account for the year ended 30 June 1989 together with extracts from the notes thereto.

Appendix 2 ACT Examination Questions

Table A2.8 Speculative PLC: profit and loss account for the year ended 30.6.91 (£)

Sales		25,580,000 [a]
Less:	Wages	(6,250,000)
	Raw materials and components	(9,600,000)
	Production overheads	(5,730,000)
	Depreciation[b]	(1,750,000)
	Interest charged[c]	(150,000)
	Other expenses[d]	(600,000)
Operating profit		1,500,000
Other income[e]		650,000
Total net profit		2,150,000

[a] Sales are estimated to increase by 10% over 1988.
[b] Depreciation is charged on a straight line basis at an average of 10% p.a. The company does not anticipate any significant change in fixed assets in the coming 2 years.
[c] The amount of interest charged to the accounts for the year is £150,000; interest of £250,000 has been capitalized representing intangible assets.
[d] The item includes £400,000 of research expenditure. Additionally, development expenditure of £250,000 has been deferred and capitalized.
[e] 'Other income' refers to the company's share in the earnings of associates. In the year ended 30 June 1989 the company received £200,000 in dividends from associates.

Treasury staff have established the following assumptions as the basis for forecasting cash flow for the year to 30 June 1990:

1 *Sales.* The total value of sales will increase by 8%.
2 *Wages.* The company plans no changes in total hours worked but wage rates are expected to increase by 12% over the year.
3 *Production overheads.* These are expected to increase in line with inflation at 7% p.a.

Appendix 2 ACT Examination Questions

4 *Raw materials and components*. These are expected to increase in value by 10%.
5 Interest and other items of income and expense are expected to remain unchanged in the coming year.

Speculative's debtors take on average 3 months to pay while it is company policy to take 2 months' credit from its suppliers of raw materials and components. All wages are paid at the end of the month to which they relate, while on average 5% of production overheads remain unpaid at the end of the year to which they relate.

Required

(a) Calculate Speculative's net cash flow for the year ended 30 June 1989 and determine the company's net liquid funds at that date.
(b) Prepare a budget of Speculative's net cash flow for the year ending 30 June 1990 from the forecast and other data given and determine whether the company will be able to meet its target overdraft facility at that date.
(c) Identify the main sources of uncertainty in the calculations in (a) and (b) above and suggest ways in which those uncertainties may be reduced and the reporting of cash flows improved.
(d) In the light of your answers to parts (a), (b) and (c) above, what advice would you give to Speculative regarding arrangements for meeting short-term funding requirements?

Answer to question 4

(a)
Cash flow for 1989, assuming sales grow by 10% over 1988.

Profit	2,150,000
+ Depreciation	1,750,000
− Capitalized interest	(250,000)
− Development expenditure	(250,000)
− Other income	(650,000)
+ Associates' dividends	200,000
	2,950,000
− Debtors $\left(\dfrac{3}{12} \times 25{,}580{,}000 \times \dfrac{0.1}{1.1}\right)$	(581,364)
+ Creditors $\left(\dfrac{2}{12} \times 9{,}600{,}000 \times \dfrac{0.1}{1.1}\right)$	145,454
+ Production overheads $\left(0.05 \times 5{,}730{,}000 \times \dfrac{0.1}{1.1}\right)$	26,045
	2,540,135
− Capex (= Depreciation)	(1,750,000)
	790,135

Therefore net liquid position at 30 June 1989

Opening cash	(3,545,255)
+ cash flow	790,135
	(2,755,120)

Appendix 2 ACT Examination Questions

(b)
Sales	25,580,000 × 1.08 =	27,626,400
Wages	6,250,000 × 1.12 =	7,000,000
Raw materials	9,600,000 × 1.10 =	10,560,000
Production overheads	5,730,000 × 1.07 =	6,131,100
Interest (cash)	=	400,000
Other expenses (cash)	=	850,000

Therefore cash flow for 1990

Sales	27,626,400
less current year debtors	(6,906,600)
plus prior year debtors	6,395,000
Wages	(7,000,000)
Raw materials	(10,560,000)
plus current year creditors	1,760,000
less prior year creditors	(1,600,000)
Production overheads	(6,131,100)
plus current year creditors	306,555
less prior year creditors	(286,500)
Interest paid	(400,000)
Other expenses	(850,000)
Associate dividend received	200,000
	2,553,755
− Capex (= depreciation)	(1,750,000)
	803,755

Therefore forecast net cash position at 30.6.90

Opening position	(2,755,120)
+ cash flow	803,755
	(1,951,365)

Appendix 2 ACT Examination Questions

Therefore, on the basis of the information provided, Speculative should be able to meet its overdraft limit of £2.2 million by 30.6.90.

(c)
Main sources of uncertainty:

1. Sustainability of sales forecasts. The high level of wages and overheads will limit room for manœuvre if sales grow more slowly than forecast.
   (a) Control this by quick reporting of sales with reliable forecasts. Can control total cash, by cutting wage costs early and by limiting capital expenditure.
2. Bad debts, stability of receipt patterns.
   (a) Control by tight chasing of overdue payments and by limiting credit available to each debtor.
3. Is the cash flow seasonal?
   (a) Control by preparing planned cash flow.
4. Are there tax and dividend payments?
   (a) If so these must be forecast and the implications for the limit controlled.
5. Wages and raw materials are growing faster than sales. If sustained this will increase borrowing requirements.
   (a) Can we bring in price increases earlier than cost increases?
   (b) Phase wage rise.
   (c) Cut capex.
6. Interest rates.
   (a) Control with fixed-rate borrowings/FRAs/options.

(d)
Essentially, Speculative needs more sources of borrowings than overdraft. In particular, a committed 2-year line would reduce the dependence on the overdraft.

Appendix 2 ACT Examination Questions

Other sources to consider include:

- factoring;
- leasing fixed assets;
- sell the associate stake.

Overall, the need to ensure the sustainability of cash generation is essential. The continuation of capitalization and the inclusion of associates' profit will show profit levels greatly in excess of actual cash generation.

Index

Absolute Return, 49–50
agent, issuing and paying, 125
annual rates, formulae, 129–30
Annualized Percentage Rates (APRs), 49–50
  formula, 50

balance reporting systems, compared with cash forecasts, 66–7
bank accounts, group organization, 62–6
bank deposits, 70–1
Bank of England, and stirling commercial paper, 78–9
banker-customer relationship, 53–5
bankers automated clearing system (BACS), 60–1
banks,
  and balance reporting systems, 66–7
  cleared balances, and problems in cash forecasts, 24–5
  products for liquidity, 56–62
basis points, 42, 122
bills of exchange, 73, 80, 122
borrowing, effect of interest rates on, example, 102–5
borrowing instruments, 75–81
  bills of exchange, 80
  commercial paper, 78–9
  marginal sources of liquidity, 80
  obtaining, 81
  overdrafts, 76–7
  sterling bankers' acceptances, 79–80

call deposits, 71
caps, 89–91, 94, 95
cash, 58–9

Index

cash book, and cash forecasts, 24–5
cash forecasts,
  and banker-customer relationship, 54–5
  compared with balance reporting systems, 66–7
  deviations from, 29–37
  importance, 9–13
  opening position, 27–8
  preparation, 9–24
    example, 10–12
    receipts and payments method, 14–19: example, 134–5; formats, 16, 18; limitations, 19
    source and application method, 19–23: examples, 142–3, 151–2; format, 21
    use of combined methods, 23–4
  problems in, 24–7
  rationalisation between subsidiaries, 26
  uses, 13–14
Certificates of Deposit (CD), 71–2, 75, 122
cheques, 57–8
clearing, 122–3, 127
clearing house automated payment system (CHAPS), 60–1
collars, 89–91, 94

commercial paper (CP), 72–3, 74–5, 78–9, 123
compound interest, effect on yield curve, 43, 45–7
credit cards, 59
credit ratings, 72–3, 79
credit risk, 44, 123

debit cards, 59
deposit instruments, 69–75
  bank deposits, 70–1
  bills of exchange, 73
  Certificates of Deposit, 71–2
  commercial paper, 72–3
  government bonds, 72
  local authority bonds, 72
  trade in, 74–5
deposit policy, and liquidity management, example, 116
destocking, and liquidity management, example, 133
direct debits, 61
disaggregation, 45–7, 84–5
  example, 103
  formula, 46–7

efficient market hypothesis, and yield curve, 47–8
engineering, and liquidity management, examples, 7–8, 109–11

facilities, committed and

Index

uncommitted, 77–8
factoring, 25, 36, 80, 124, 133
financial futures, 87–8, 124
floors, 89–91, 94
foreign currency,
   currency risk, 13–14, 17, 73–4
   and exchange rates assumptions, 25–6
   and interest-rate calculation, 40
forward forward interest rates, 84–5
Forward Rate Agreements (FRAs),
   and financial futures, 88
   and hedging instruments, 94, 95, 96
   and interest rates, 85–7 example, 86–7
   use of, example, 104
futures, 94, 124

government bonds, 72, 124

hedging, 124
hedging instruments, and interest rate, 94–6

interest periods, choice of, 42–8
interest rates,
   assumptions, and problems in cash forecasts, 25–6
   and cash forecasts, 13–14

and Certificates of Deposit, 71
effect on borrowing, example, 102–5
exposure, 125
and liquidity management, example, 117
risk, example, 136–7
and risk management,
   caps, floors and collars, 89–91
   Forward Rate Agreements, 85–7: example, 86–7
   hedging instruments, 94–6
   implications of changes, 83–4
   options, 91–4: example, 93–4
   swaps, 88–9
   structure of, 39–51
international trade, and banks' services, 61–2
invoice discounting, 125

letter of credit, irrevocable, 123, 125
LIBOR (London inter-bank offered rate), 41–2, 125
liquidity,
   circumstances, 2–3, 4–6
   defined, 1
   forecasting, 9–28
   sources of, 34–6
liquidity management,

Index

liquidity management, (*cont'd.*)
  objectives, 1–2, 3–4
  organization of, 115–20
    treasury committee, 117–20
    in practice: examples; 98–113; flow chart, 99
liquidity preference, effect on yield curve, 44
local authority bonds, 72

manufacturing, and liquidity management, examples, 131–7, 145–54
money transmission, bank products for, 56–62
money-markets, 126
money-markets, wholesale, 39–40
multinational corporation, and liquidity management, example, 112–13

netting, and organization of group banks accounts, 62–6

options, 126
  and hedging instruments, 94, 95
  on interest rates, 91–4
    examples, 93–4, 112

overdrafts, 76–7

performance measurement, 51

relationship banking, 54
risk, and interest rates, 48, example, 136–7

strike price, 92–3
swaps, 88–9
  and hedging instruments, 94, 95
  and options, example, 112

taxation, 96
telegraphic transfers, 59–61
trade terms, 80
transaction banking, 54
treasury committee, 117–20

uncertainty, management of, 29–37

variables, in cash forecasts, 33–4
variance analysis, 30–3

yield curve,
  and interest periods, 42–8
  interpretation, 47–8

zero-balancing, and organization of group banks accounts, 64–6